ARTHUR RAISTRICK'S YORKSHIRE DALES

Winter at Arncliffe   M'Duke Miller

The Ribble, near Stainforth   Godfrey Wilson

ARTHUR RAISTRICK'S YORKSHIRE DALES

compiled by David Joy

Dalesman Books

The Dalesman Publishing Company Ltd,
Clapham, Lancaster, LA2 8EB

First published 1991
© Arthur Raistrick 1991

ISBN: 1 85568 035 1

Typeset by Lands Services, East Molesey, Surrey
Printed by Biddles Ltd, Guildford, Surrey

CONTENTS

Foreword   7

Arthur Raistrick   11

Dales Life and Landscape
    Pack-Horse Ways   19
    Dew-Ponds   26
    Dolly of Kimpergill   30
    Forests of the Dales   34
    The Thorn Tree   41

Crafts and Industry
    Besom Makers of the Dales   45
    Pennine Peat Pits   52
    Yorkshire Stone   57
    Story of the Limekiln   63
    Water Power in the Dales   75

Buildings of the Dales
    Dales Building of the Sixteenth
    and Seventeenth Centuries
        1. Bridges   87
        2. Cottages   92
        3. Smaller Halls 99
        4. Farms   106
        5. Schools   112
    Barden Tower   117
    Norton Tower   124

Mining and the Dales Miner

Silver Mines in the Dales   131

Lead from the Grey Hills   134

Water Wheels at the Mines   140

Life in the Lead Mines   144

Spirit of the Dales

 153

Index

 155

The publishers acknowledge the kindness of
Ken Howarth, Sound Archivist of
the North West Sound Archive, Clitheroe,
in making available the transcript from which
the material on pages 11 to 16 has been extracted.

As acknowledged on page 154, the article "Spirit of the Dales" is taken from *Open Fell Hidden Dale* by permission of John & Eliza Forder. All other material in the book has previously appeared in the *Dalesman* (or the Dalesman's *Yorkshire Annual*), the date of original publication being given at the end of each extract.

FOREWORD

WE at the *Dalesman* owed much to Arthur Raistrick, who died in April 1991. He was one of our first contributors. In time of war, when paper was rationed, we devoted much space to his long, learned but never dull articles about Dales life. They gave the magazine an authentic flavour.

Arthur did not expect a fee for the articles, nor for the series, such as that on dry-stone walling, which was eventually to be re-published as the first *Dalesman* book. It has gone through umpteen editions and continues to sell.

We are privileged to use manuscripts that were a consequence of consulting original sources and of his own deep experience of the Dales in field and on fell, not just as a scholar working in his study at his home at Linton-on-Craven.

Arthur had a distinguished career at King's College, Newcastle, retiring as Reader. He was later to receive honorary doctorates from the universities of Leeds and Bradford.

His wife Elizabeth predeceased him by many years; she, too, was a notable historian who had the ability to express her research well, as evidenced by a series we published on home life in the Dales through the centuries. It was Elizabeth who wrote us a book about village schools in Wharfedale and who – when I called on baking day – gave me coffee, plus some fresh buttered scones!

The House had been a large Dales barn. Typically, Elizabeth wrote us an article about its conversion, and also sent photographs.

As far as I can recall, he never visited the offices of the *Dalesman*, though he was our most respected author. Visiting him at Linton was always stimulating. He usually had something of interest to show me and once I found the living room almost papered with lead-mining photographs, from which he was making a selection for a book based on the Beamish collection.

He was a meticulous field worker. I remember seeing him, in old age, standing by an excavation on the moor near Threshfield, saying little but making each word count. He ignored the discomfort of a spirited Pennine breeze that was blowing his white hair about like the locks of an Old Testament prophet.

As a Quaker, he was a regular attender at Meeting and also, in his daily life, a man of upright character. He carried his Quakerism into his research, as with his books relating to a Quaker concern, the London Lead Company, which had transformed the North Pennine mining field and also the everyday lives of the miners. *(Quakers in Science and Industry; Dynasty of Ironfounders)*.

Arthur rose early, played his much-loved gramophone records of classical music for an hour or so, and then settled down to work. He went early to bed. He made his mark as a geologist, engineer, industrial archaeologist, historian, field researcher and excavator, author, socialist, photographer, rambler and lecturer. He was faithful over many years to several worthy causes, such as the Ramblers' Association and the Holiday Fellowship, being president of both organisations. He was a supporter, worker for and defender of the National Park movement, as well as an informed critic of the work of the various Park authorities.

To catalogue Arthur's work would be to induce writer's cramp. He was the author of 39 books and over 150 pamphlets and learned articles. He was the friend of Mine Research organisations and keenly interested in the efforts made to consolidate what was left of mining history. He wrote books on aspects of the Dales that had previously been under-researched. He devised the discipline of industrial archaeology. The high standard he set for recording local history will be a measure against which future work is evaluated.

Happily, he lived long enough for many of his ambitions in the realm of science and historical research to be fulfilled. A friend and regular companion said of Arthur Raistrick's passing that it was akin to the closing of a vast encyclopaedia, which could never be reopened. Through the legacy of his writings we can take at least a glimpse into parts of that encyclopaedic mind and unique personality.

W.R. Mitchell
(editor of *The Dalesman*, 1968-1988)

Littondale   M'Duke Miller

Fountains Abbey from the West   Dennis Mallet

ARTHUR RAISTRICK

(in conversation with Ken Howarth of the North West Sound Archive)

KH: You were born in Saltaire? Which is an interesting community by itself isn't it?

AR: Very interesting, and I enjoyed it because my mother and my aunts and three of my uncles were all working in the mill, so that there was a lot of talk at home and in the family about what went on. I found that most of the people we knew in Saltaire were very proud of it because when I was a young child Titus Salt and his wife were about and took an interest in the people in the village as they called it. So we really knew a lot about them.

KH: Your early education – where did you go to school?

AR: I went to elementary school in Shipley, then with a scholarship to Bradford Grammar School.

KH: It wasn't long after you left school, I suppose, that the war started. The first war.

AR: Well, yes. I left school in 1912 and was apprenticed at the Shipley Electricity Works. I served my apprenticeship until 1915 when the war had started, and then what we call the Derby Scheme came along which gave you a badge if you were in important work. I refused mine in engineering, of course, I had to leave.

KH: Why did you refuse?

AR: Well it was part of the war organisation which I refused to have anything to do with. My uncle and I spent the greater part of a year round about the north of England, tramping about and speaking on peace. We did a lot with Ramsay MacDonald. My father had been a founder member of the Independent Labour Party. The first thing I clearly remember was the 1902 conference in Bradford which finalised it and there Ramsay MacDonald joined them and Bernard Shaw. I remember them coming and speaking at that committee, and then later on we knew Philip Snowden very well personally and Keir Hardy. They used to stay with us if they were in the district. My uncle and I spent that part of 1915 at pacifist meetings.

KH: Did you every meet any official sort of resentment from, say, the police-force, official pressures?

AR: No, they were reasonable, we were just cranks and it was best to leave us alone. We met some man-handling now and again but we didn't mind – we were used to it. Some of our meetings were broken up by the police from time to time. It was a very interesting time. Very good for me as a young lad. And then, of course, my uncle and I were both arrested.

KH: How did this arise?

AR: Well because we were both of military service age and had got our call-up papers which we simply returned to them crossed out, put great black crosses and sent them back to the military so that we were arrested as deserters. Went to the police courts.

KH: How did they actually arrest you? Where did you go?

AR: Oh they, the police were waiting at home one time when I came home from a series of meetings. I went first to the military barracks at Halifax, there for a while, then at the military barracks in York. Refused to do anything so of course we were in cells for a long time there, then eventually court-martialled. Went to Wormwood Scrubs for a year's sentence there, and then court-martialled again and was in Durham nearly two years until September 1919.

KH: What sort of treatment did you have before you went to prison?

AR: There was a lot of ill treatment, knocking about and dragging about the parade ground and that sort of thing. They marched you out with the recruits and gave orders which you just disobeyed. When they said "right turn" or whatever it might be, you just didn't and very often they told the soldiers next to you to "turn that man round." It was done as roughly as possible and occasionally one was knocked down and dragged about the ground. You just refused to do anything, you wouldn't have anything to do with the military.

KH: What about the general conditions that you were kept in at Durham?

AR: They were the ordinary prison conditions. Twenty minutes' exercise each day, and rather short ration, no talking of course, but after you'd been in a year you were allowed what was called association – that is you sat nicely spaced out in the prison hall doing your mail-bag sewing. You could see other people and that was quite a concession. You had your letter once a month that was heavily censored. It was hard but one adapted to it.

KH: When you were finally released from prison, what happened then?

AR: I'd got a scholarship while I was working as an apprentice – a West Riding Major for Leeds University. So I went to Leeds and took Civil Engineering. I stayed there until I graduated, then I stayed on and took geology with Professor Kendal. Stayed on and took a Ph.D.

KH: And from there . . .?

AR: Well from there I was unemployable under that curious regulation against conscientious objectors. But I took on some research work for Kendal for a year, then I got a Royal Society grant and one from the Mine Owners' Association and I worked for many years underground in collieries all over the country studying abnormalities of coal seams.

KH: So what happened at the end of that very long period?

AR: Well I was lecturing in Kings College as it then became. I'd turned over much more to mining. I did a lot of work in the Alston Moor mines and some in Teesdale, working first with Professor Louis and then with Poole who followed him. And running a lot of Saturday afternoon and evening classes for miners, very big classes, working for the Deputy certificates and that sort of thing. That was my main occupation out of college.

KH: That period was rapidly approaching the second world war?

AR: Yes, that was so. I was busy then with the Pacifist Advisory Bureau for the north. Charles and Mary Trevelyan and myself and one or two others founded it to help young pacifists. Attended a lot of the court trials on their behalf. The Ministry of Supply then wanted to register all the people concerned with engineering for their use in munitions. I refused that registration and I wouldn't have ought to do with it. College just had to suspend me, so I was suspended without salary from 1939. I came and made this house at Linton, Wharfedale, from an old barn and lived down here. I took the old hospital garden – about quarter of an acre that wasn't used, and we lived on that and what I could do in this part of the field. In 1945 I was invited to take a Fellowship at the Quaker College, Woodbrook, Selly Oak. I went there, and while I was there I was invited by Newcastle to go back and make a department of mining engineering, so I finished my Fellowship at Woodbrook and then went back to Newcastle. Stayed there until 1956, when the Vice Chancellor, who was a friend, asked if I could be allowed to retire at sixty instead of sixty-five so that I could go on to the National Park Committee. I was already on the Bootham and Mount School Committees at York, and Ayton Friends School – too busy to work! So I left college then and I went on to the standing committee on National Parks and the Yorkshire Dales National Park Committee.

KH: Well, the Yorkshire Dales – how did you first become attracted to them?

AR: I was born to them that's why. I was born in Airedale. My grandfather on my mother's side came from Swaledale and her mother was a Redmire woman. My grandmother on the other side was a Wharfedale woman, and my grandfather there was an Airedale man so I had four grandparents from four Dales. We were an ordinary working class family, we didn't go away for holidays, but as a boy at school I used to go and spend a lot of my holidays with a variety of cousins and half-cousins up and down all the Dales, so that I can't remember when I didn't know the Dales.

KH: You were saying to me earlier that you don't in fact drive. How on earth did you get around the Dales in those days?

drovers?

AR: Largely walking. My uncles were all harriers, and my father – a thing I never hear of nowadays. They always did a great deal of walking. When I was ten I used to go on the annual Bradford to York walk and when we went out to see my relations in Wensleydale we always walked there from Bradford. We walked over to Nelson from Bradford; I never remember riding to Nelson. We very often took holidays... we were all used to rough sleeping out of doors, sleeping in barns and that, and we'd go over and see our relations in Swaledale on our holiday – walk it all, and I've kept that up. That's why I suppose I became President of the Ramblers' Association.

KH: So, when and why did you feel you wanted to write about the Dales?

AR: I think from my very many W.E.A. classes up and down the Dales. I started a lot of the W.E.A. work up here where the other tutors wouldn't come. I was at first so shocked that the local people didn't know their own district in detail – and they ought to – and then to find how delighted they were to hear about its history, natural history and industrial history. And they were so stuck, these two reactions of mine to my students, that I first wrote that *Teach Yourself Geology* for them, to give them a basis. Then I wrote a lot with Harry Scott – I was associated with him when he started the *Dalesman* you see. He was turned off the *Manchester Guardian* during the war, and came to Clapham with Edward Seal, an artist. Harry said he would run the *Dalesman* if Ted Seal vetted the art and I wrote some articles for him. I began writing there, and so many people wrote to me how they wanted to know and were learning more about the Dales. I thought well, I'd better write it up. So I started then. My first book was *The London Lead Company*, and that came from my mining history and my association with Alston Moor and the long history of the Lead Company and my interest in Quaker history.

KH: I know having been to one of your lectures recently that you urge people to record. Why?

AR: Because most of our knowledge has got to come, if it's been recorded, from the records whatever form they may take. Whether they're archival, or whether they're verbal, or whether they're the study of the actual remains, it's a matter of interpretation. The interpretation can only come either as a romanticism in the way you would look at and write about an old castle ruin, or a scientific investigation which almost certainly involves either clearance of a site or archaeological excavations and study along with a knowledge of technology of the time.

KH: And you have yourself done a great deal of research into the lead mining industry?

AR: Yes a great deal, including quite a lot of archaeological survey and excavations.

KH: I remember when you were talking about the various water courses. You mentioned that your own experiences as an engineer have been particularly helpful.

Clouds over Kilnsey   Dan Binns

AR: Yes, I was looking at them as an engineer, and although they'd been there nobody else had looked at them. But there were many problems about them, about levels and interchange and that sort of thing, that could only be solved by digging them out and studying their junctions. It was an archaeological matter and I spread it, weekends, over a couple of years probably.

KH: Having talked about your writing, talked about your work, what did you do for leisure?

AR: Well that was my leisure.

KH: No hobbies?

AR: No, and I've never had any games experience at all. The whole of my life has been so spent – starting with my grandfather who was a great walker and a Dalesman and who, when I was a boy, advised me: "Lad," he says, "pick the area and get to know it."

DALES LIFE
AND LANDSCAPE

The Wharfe, near Appletreewick   Godfrey Wilson

PACK-HORSE WAYS

Every Dalesman, worthy of the name, must, at some time have walked with joy and gratitude along one or other of the green roads over the fells, and in his heart poured blessings on the unknown makers of such a lovable track. The way over Horsehead into Littondale; parts of the road from Settle to Malham and forward to Kilnsey; tracks from Arkengarthdale to Bowes, and similar ways between every dale and its neighbours, are known to all who frequent the fells and moors.

A winter evening spent with adequate maps will soon reveal that those many fragments of green road and bridle path can be linked up into a few continuous ways, partly incorporated in later roads; ways often crossing the whole Dales area, and traceable even further afield, suggesting that at some time in their history they have been highways of importance used by traffic to and from far places, a traffic now lost and forgotten or shifted into the valley bottoms on to new roads and railways. Pack-horse roads and bridges, drove roads, "streets" and "gates" are memorials of a time when the byways and hamlets of today had a different importance and were vital parts of the economic life of the area.

From pre-historic and Roman times we inherit two "patterns" of tracks. Firstly, the pre-Roman paths, almost certainly absorbed and preserved in many of the upland tracks along the fell edges, often passing by "camp" and hut settlement sites of the Iron Age, like beads on a continuous string. These older paths rarely cross a watershed, and only descend the valleys where the floor is rocky and free from swamp. The Roman roads are much more direct in their bold lines, cutting across the country, and using the valley sides and gaps only so far as they can be fitted into a bold long distance plan. The great road from Bainbridge over Cam Fell, the road over Blackstone Edge, and on the moors between Addingham and Blubberhouses are sufficient examples of this pattern, overlain on the country with the minimum reference to local needs and population.

The second form, the pack-horse ways, differ from these earlier road patterns in their direct relation to the economic and social life of the area and their intimate coincidence with the village pattern of the Dales. Pack-horses and ponies were the prime form of transport for approximately five centuries; largely developed in monastic times they were only finally ousted from their important position by the transport revolution of the early nineteenth century.

The monastic communities spread their economy over a wide area. Fountains Abbey held, by grant and lease, over a million acres of land in Craven, and from them drew great stocks of wool, their average yearly production, according to the list of wool exports to Italy in the thirteenth century, being nearly 28,000 lbs. weight. Bolton Priory held lands in Wharfedale and the Malham district, and Sawley Abbey had great areas in

Bowland, in Ribblesdale between Settle and Stainforth, and around Gargrave. These again were heavily committed to sheep rearing and production of wool, though in the case of Sawley, a moderate amount of corn was grown on the lower lands in Airedale. In the case of Fountains and Bolton, sheep were brought down off the fells to Kilnsey and Malham, for shearing and lambing at the respective granges, or were driven by easy stages to the Lake District for summer pasture on the abbey estates around Watendlath. The wool from the granges was carried to the Abbey, and from there to the River Ouse, probably at Clifton, York, for shipment abroad.

In addition to the wool, hides, coal, iron, lead, charcoal and peat, were carried eastward from Craven, and at some seasons, fish from Malham and from the rivers. In addition to produce from their own lands, many of the rents of monastic tenants were paid in kind, and the abbeys received many gifts of the tithe of parishes, again paid in kind. Corn and supplies of many kinds were carried back from east to west along these tracks which were paved with stones in swampy ground, and worn to deep-cut sunk ways up the hill shoulders. Crossing through an unenclosed country the tracks took the shortest practicable route, and in the course of centuries of use became stabilised as roads. One of the most important of these roads is that from Fountains Abbey by Pateley Bridge, Grassington, and the grange at Kilnsey, over the Malham fells to Stainforth with diverging routes to Settle from Malham and from Trenhouse to Helwith Bridge on the Ribble, forward then by Wharfe and Clapham to Ingleton. Parts of this road are now macadamised, and some of it has been slightly diverted during the period when it was one of the cross post roads from York to Lancaster via Knaresborough and Pateley Bridge (given in detail in Paterson's Roads, 1808, etc).

The sheep rearing and wool industry in Craven needed an army of workers, shepherds, retainers of all kinds, stewards of the granges, with men at the mines owned by the abbeys, and these were largely supplied with food and raiment from the parent house. We have no actual account of their numbers, but for a house like Fountains the dependants in Craven must have numbered some hundreds, and their supplies must have provided a constant return load for the pack trains.

After the dissolution of the monasteries the pack horse roads remained as the main ways of commerce and the pack bridges and fords were the only important crossing places on the rivers until the Turnpike Trusts found it necessary to enlarge the bridges and plan new ones. A pack-horse train was made up from 20 to 40 horses or ponies, with a driver and one or two attendants. The ponies commonly used in the North of England were imported from Germany, where they are known as Jaeger (hunter) ponies, hence our dales form of the word survives in place names like Jagger Lane, Jagger Hill, or in the surname Jagger, often given to the pack drain drivers and attendants. Each pony carried a pair of panniers or a wooden pack saddle, or if bales of wool or some other light but bulky load was being transported, a wooden frame, called a crutch, was fixed over the pony's back, in which a sack could rest on each side.

The normal load of a pack pony was two and a quarter hundred-weights, and loads are generally measured in units or multiples of this. Panniers and saddles were of different sizes according to the bulk of the load carried, but approximated to the normal load in weight when filled. Thus large panniers were used for charcoal and peat, and much smaller ones for ore or coal. Lead at the smelt mills was usually cast in "pieces" of approximately eight stones weight, two pieces being a sufficient load for a pony, and quite sufficient for comfort, to have hanging against its sides. The making of panniers was quite an important subsidiary craft, practiced mainly in the east and south of Yorkshire, though there were a few basket and pannier makers in Craven and East Lancashire. Baskets for charcoal and peat cost 7/- and 8/- a dozen in 1720, while the much smaller but tighter weave baskets for iron ore and coal cost 2/- or 2/6 a dozen.

The leading pony in a pack train had a harness of bells, whose music marked the leader and kept the following ponies together. It is said that the bells of the leader were also needed to give warning of the approach at awkward places where the roads were only deep sunk tracks, too narrow for two trains to pass. The children of Yorkshire still preserved a tradition of this in my boyhood, when they played "bell-horses", by running in large numbers in tandem, with one or two "drivers" and the leading horse always called the "bell-horse", a position for which there was great competition. Even fights and rough-and-tumble jostling by rival teams probably had their origin in remembrance of such disputes when pack-horses met in an awkward place and each refused to give way to the other. The pack-horse bells were of iron or brass, spherical with a small slit on the underside and a loose piece of metal inside, similar to the small bells still found on children's toy reins.

Among the pack-horse carriers, as in all later forms of transport, there were many grades in the scale of business; many small men had only three or four ponies, while the larger concerns often ran several trains of 30 or 40 horses in each. The mining companies, the larger clothiers and the potters probably maintained the greater part of the full-sized trains. In the mid-eighteenth century, a hundred and fifty horses a week provided a regular service between Manchester and Bewdley or Bridgnorth, on the Severn, carrying cotton and woollen cloth for export via Bristol. These services were organised in regular "gangs" of 30 horses, with a driver and two attendants. An advert in "Leeds Mercury", June 1728, is as follows: "A Gang of Good Pack-horses, containing eighteen in number, with their accoutrements and Business belonging to the same, being one of the ancient gangs that has gone with Goods from York, Leeds, and Wakefield to London, being the Horses of Thomas Varley . . ." etc., are for sale. Nearly the whole output of the Staffordshire potteries, prior to the making of the canals, was distributed over the country by smaller trains of five to ten horses.

Wool was collected and also taken for combing, spinning and weaving to remote farmhouses and villages all over the Pennines, and cloth was carried to the markets and to the dyers and finishers, by pack-horse. In the proposals for a canal to connect with the Leeds and Liverpool Canal, in 1776, it is stated that 30 pack-horses a week travelled between Settle and Kendal with wool, yarn, and cloth, and that a greater number were employed between Settle, Skipton, Leeds and Halifax. The canal would hasten the journey and reduce the cost.

The mines at Grassington sent their lead and silver from the smelt mills to Gargrave, Skipton and Leeds by pack-horse train, bringing back coal and stores, while at an earlier period mines from all over the Dales area sent their lead to the great lead markets at Kirkby Malzeard or Yarm. The roads made by this traffic can still be traced over most of the remoter moorlands of the dales.

From every mine the ore was carried by pony to the appropriate smelt mill, and stores were brought to the mine from the villages and market towns. In Bastow Wood, Grassington, there are many walled and turfed enclosures that were made during the seventeenth and early eighteenth centuries by miners, who in return for looking after the pack ponies were allowed to enclose these small crofts for themselves and cultivate the ground.

The cost of the transport by pack-horse was fairly high, averaging in the Midlands and Potteries as much as a shilling per ton per mile, or on long runs eight shillings per ton for ten miles. The charges were different in winter and summer, owing to the vast difference in the ease of travelling and the different lengths of the day. On a long journey the ponies had to be rested each night at a place where they could feed, and attendants and sometimes outside helpers were needed to unload the packs and repack in the morning. Wayside inns, farmhouses, and houses, sometimes maintained by the mines or the carrier concerns, provided enclosed pasturage or stabling for the ponies and entertainment for the men. Along frequent routes there was often difficulty in getting sufficient eatage or fodder for the ponies, and prices for accommodation were increased. In the northern coal fields several petitions against the increased prices of coal were answered by the charge that pack-horse carriers were putting up their charges because of the high price of feeding for the ponies, now that natural pasturage was all eaten up. In the lead mining areas of the Dales, several complaints were made of the difficulty of providing enough pasturage along the roadsides for the ponies, and charges of allowing ponies to trespass in search of cheap food were numerous. Sometimes, as on the pack trains carrying lead and silver from the mines, or packmen with costly materials, guards would accompany the train, and on some routes where this was customary, small guard houses were maintained. Most of the pack-horse roads in Craven have houses or ruins of houses alongside that flourished on the custom of the pack trains.

A fine example of the pack-horse house is seen at Dalehead, under the shelter of Penyghent, near the crossing of two pack-horse ways, Stainforth – Halton Gill – Yockenthwaite – Middleham, and Kilnsey – Malham – Horton – Ribblehead – Dent. The junction of the two ways is also marked by the remains of a wayside cross, the socket stone similar to those found along most of the monastic ways. There are several on the side of the Kilnsey – Stainforth track and many built into walls in various parts of the Dales. Fine examples still stand at Rere Cross and Grains 'o Beck, on Stainmoor, and the site of others is preserved in place names such as Craven Cross (Greenhow), Stump Cross, Acre Cross, etc. The crosses marked the boundaries of monastic lands, or in many cases were put up to mark and consecrate the way.

The pack-horse ways come down to the rivers and streams where they are narrow enough for a single span bridge, or where there is a hard stony ford. The pack bridges have a narrow way, often between parapets sufficiently low to allow the passage above them of the panniers and packs. In some cases the parapets have been added at a time subsequent to the building of the bridge. Every dalesman knows the pack bridge at Stainforth (Stony-ford) on Ribble, and Ivelet on Swale, but most of our surviving pack bridges are over tributary streams, the main rivers being too wide for a single span, and being crossed by a ford. Occasionally the two-span early bridge is incorporated in the modern bridge and can be seen underneath, as at the main road bridges at Gigglewick and Kildwick.

Smaller pack bridges are surprisingly beautiful in their simplicity and strength; the bridge over Ling Gill near Ribblehead, on the old pack-horse way, Settle – Horton – High Birkwith – Cam End-Hawes, is one of the simplest. Others are found in all parts of the Dales, some of them often recorded in photograph or painting ("Yorks. Dalesman" Vol. I, No. 12 has a photo of the Washburn bridge). Some of the larger bridges along the pack-horse ways were of wood until the seventeenth or early eighteenth century, when they were rebuilt in stone, at the expense of a general levy on the county.

Besides the local economy of the Dales area, two great traffics linked up the pack-horse roads with regions far beyond the confines of the Pennines – those of cattle and salt. Of the cattle, sheep, and horse fairs, many have long since disappeared and the roads connected with them are now forgotten. The Malham sheep fair in October, dating probably from monastic times, developed in the eighteenth century into a great cattle and sheep fair lasting several weeks, and visited by drovers from Scotland, who spent many weeks on the journey driving their stock along the green roads and pack ways, by Clennel Street over the Cheviots, and by drove roads right down the Pennine summits, slowly converging on Malham Moor. Along these drove ways there are several ruined inns and rest houses, one at Malham stands just within Great Close, where the fair was held; Middle House and its maze of small closes round it is typical of many of the resting places along the way. Gearstones, near Ribblehead, was on the way by Dentdale from The Howgills and the Lake District, and had an ancient market for corn and oatmeal, brought largely from Wensleydale and sold to drovers and visiting dealers from Dentdale and Ingleton districts. Many now isolated and ruined places were then important markets and fairs, or inns and calling places when the pack-horse roads were the commercial highways of the dales.

Salt was the prime necessity for the preserving of winter meat, until the introduction of winter fodder for cattle enabled stock to be carried over from one year to the next. Prior to that most cattle not needed for breeding were killed and the meat salted down in early November, and for this many stones of salt were needed in each household. It was brought from the "salt-pans" on the coast, or from the Cheshire and South Lancashire salt areas, carried by pack-horses along the "salt-ways." The salt-ways radiate out from south Lancashire across the Pennines, intersecting or linking on to the more local pack-horse roads. Salt-way place names are abundant, particularly south of Airedale – Salterforth and Salter Hebble mark fords on the salt-ways, Salters Gate, Salter Lane, Salter Rake, etc., are frequently repeated along these ways.

If on some fine moonlit night we could see the ghosts of these old users of the green roads passing along them once more, what a procession we should enjoy – monk and drover, collier, charcoal burner and shepherd, salter and packman from the distant fairs, would throng by with pack ponies whose panniers held a surprising range of goods: coal, charcoal, salt, wool, and hides, perhaps would be the bulkiest; cloth, grain, small domestic ware, wooden utensils and crockery, with lead, silver, and ironware, and in the packman's or "chapman's" packs, silks, ribbons, cheap jewellery, spices and comfits, and small drapery from far distant fairs.

Along the lowland and eastward tracks between the coastal markets such as Boston and Hull and York, and the monastic houses, we should watch a traffic of wines, vestments, parchments and books, for the abbeys with delicacies for the abbot's table and lodgings, returning after the carriage of wool and lead for export to France and Italy. Macadam and Stephenson and their armies have changed all that, and drawn the traffic to the valley bottoms, leaving the highways of the fells and moors for the wandering dalesman and the hiker. Let us value our heritage all the more for the busy past it has known, in contrast with its present grateful solitude.

(March 1941)

Penyghent   John F. Greenwood

DEW-PONDS:
or why Jack and Jill went *up* the Hill

"We have no waters to delight our broad and brookless vales –
Only the dew-pond on the height unfed, that never fails,
Whereby no tattered herbage tells which way the season flies –
Only our close-bit thyme that smells like dawn in Paradise."

Such is Kipling's description of part of the Sussex Downs, and the words will apply without alteration to parts of west and north Yorkshire. On many of the broad stretches of limestone pasture that lie round the head of the dales, over most of Craven and a good part of Wensleydale the dew-pond is a familiar sight. A shallow bowl-shaped depression three of four yards in diameter, and possibly two or three feet deep at its centre, circular, and now mostly grass-grown, the typical dew-pond is stumbled across in many a quiet hollow on the fells. Occasionally the pond is really a pond with a pool of water to which faint sheep tracks lead from a good distance round about. In a few cases the hollow stares blankly skyward in a dry circle of grey concrete, with grass and nettles growing out of its many cracks.

The name "dew-pond" is only of mid-nineteenth century origin though the ponds are often of considerable antiquity; writers have been happy to wrap the ponds in mystery, to ascribe them to the work of craftsmen whose art has long been lost, and to relate their capacity for containing water in the driest season, to some mysterious property not now understood.

Dew-ponds are common on the Chalk Downs of England, and on some of the areas of thick limestone – in fact on any upland where the nature and structure of the rock is such that the normal drainage is by underground and not surface streams. The problem of watering sheep and cattle on such areas which are generally areas of fine pasture, has existed from the earliest time when man tried to domesticate sheep or to live himself on these dry uplands. Associated with many of the earthworks, "camps" and village sites of prehistoric times on the Downs, there are ponds, mostly now dry, on some of which ancient cattle and sheep paths as well as habitation sites, converge. On our limestone pastures of Craven, ancient dew-ponds are abundant in the areas of Iron Age and Romano-British camps, and so frequent is the coincidence of them, that we are almost justified in regarding them as part and parcel of the same culture. There are of course many dew-ponds of fairly recent construction as well as of intermediate ages, sufficient to suggest a very long continuity of their use and construction.

When closely examined (several have been partially excavated both for examination and for repair) they are found to consist essentially of the bowl-shaped hollow cut in the soil and subsoil, usually in the middle of an area of shallow depression which may extend to a few acres. The hollow is lined with thick clay puddle well trampled into position. In the very few references we have made to dew-ponds, it is clear that the common way was to carry up clay for puddle, spread it over the hollow and then "temper" it by driving cattle back and forth across it until the whole was worked into a first class waterproof bed. To prevent the cattle hooves doing damage to the puddle skin while it was being formed, straw or rushes were generally thrown in with the clay to form a tough mat. In the course of a comparatively short time, the straw decays, and plays no real part in the final efficiency of the pond. To protect the puddle after the pond comes into use, the whole hollow is paved out with large stones right to the edge of the clay and a little beyond. In the abandoned ponds this pavement is often to be seen under the grass cover that now fills them.

The name dew-pond was given in the mid-nineteenth century because it was then thought that all the water that collected in the pond was received directly by the deposition of a heavy dew over the pond area. This simple explanation is not sufficient and recent investigations suggest a multiple source for the water. When the pond has been properly made, it is found that during the drier summer months, the pond will often receive four or five inches depth of water during a still, clear night, and will maintain a useful level of water even through prolonged drought, when all other sources fail. The position of the dew-pond in a natural hollow however shallow, ensures that what little rain does fall, drains into the pond and is thus saved. During very hot weather, the evaporation of moisture from the earth is great during the day, and at night the air has a high water vapour content. There is a certain temperature, called the dew-point, at which the atmosphere will cease to hold all the water vapour it contains, and some of it will be condensed on cold surfaces as dew. On a clear cloudless night following a clear day of heat, radiation of heat from the surface of the ground will be at a maximum. Where a dew-pond is in good condition, the puddled circle acts as an insulator preventing the radiation of heat from its area, and so remains, in comparison with the surrounding ground, a cold spot. Over this cold spot air currents tend to descend and flow outwards at ground level, and a considerable flowage may be set up. If the air is already near the dew-point it is nearly saturated with water vapour which can condense on the cold spot around the pond, and so renew supplies. Any objects round the pond – low thorn bushes are fairly frequent, heaps of stones, thick grass – will all help condensation of dew, and a moderate amount of water will be obtained in this way. When weather conditions are such that low cloud or mist lies on the fells, these "cold-spot" hollows will tend to hold cloud and mist longer than other parts – indeed I have frequently seen the remnants of heavy Scotch mist flowing down the sides of a hollow and accumulating over a dew-pond site. Again the drenching condensation from such a mist drains into the area of the pond and may refill it on a day when the lower ground has had no rain at all. The supplies are thus drawn in part from heavy dews, from condensation of mists, and from the rains falling in the small drainage area of the pond.

When a pond is old and neglected, grass will grow in the crannies between the paving, the roots penetrate the puddle and allow the escape of water, and the pond dries out. The cracking of the puddle soon follows, and the pond changes from a dew-pond to a wet weather pool, and before long even the wettest weather fails to maintain a pool in what has become an upland seive. During the last forty years many farmers have resorted to concrete as a convenient waterproofing, but a thin skim of concrete has only inferior insulation value compared with the thick puddle and stone, and, sooner rather than later, frost will crack the concrete and destroy the value of the pond.

Of the West Yorkshire dew-ponds there is a small proportion that by their very close association with the Iron Age camps can safely be referred to that age, though none of these is still known by me to be in use. There are many finely built larger diameter stone-paved ponds of the sixteenth and seventeenth centuries, when sheep pasturage came into its own. Many of these were made before or during the Enclosure walling, as walls frequently diverge from the direct line in order to pass over a dew-pond and so give water to two enclosures. Occasional boundary ridings refer to dew-ponds as boundary marks in the seventeenth century.

Whatever be the date of the dew-ponds, they will always have an air of mystery and will carry the mind back to the dim past when some observant Neolithic cattleman noticed that when his cattle puddled the ground at a camp entrance or near an occasional spring, the hollow so formed, held water after rain. Generations must have used cattle puddled hollows before the daring idea of making an "artificial" puddle was born. The final working out of the art of making dew-ponds extended through periods for which we have no written history but only folk memory and tradition. The old nursery rhyme, Jack and Jill went *up* the hill to fetch a pail of water, has always seemed wrong. It is general experience, ever since the settlement of most of our villages, that people go *down* the hill to the springs or rivers for water. If Jack and Jill were members of an Iron Age hillside community, they would certainly avoid the boggy, danger-infested valley bottom, and climb the limestone scars uphill to dip their pail in the hilltop dew-pond. We shall never know, but it may not be too absurd to think that Jack and Jill were early prototypes of our dales shepherd folk, and that they could probably have told us much about the making of dew-ponds that all our research today fails to reveal.

(November 1944)

Grassington Roofs   John F. Greenwood

DOLLY of Kimpergill

Among the generations of Grassington folk now almost passed away, there used to be many tales of odd characters and queer doings which were told at the fireside, particularly in the family gatherings held during the Feast week. Of these stories, one which is now almost entirely forgotten, concerned an old woman called Dolly Gill who occupied a solitary cottage some way outside the present village of Grassington. She was remembered even then as something of a "character," who, among other eccentricities, always wore a great red cloak, and was no doubt thought to be in some measure a white witch or wise-woman.

One winter, the story goes, the district experienced a snow storm of unusual severity during which many sheep were trapped on the hills and high pastures and all Grassington's men were kept hard at work rescuing sheep or trying to keep open the roads and dressing floors of some of the mines.

Dolly's cottage stood in a deepish little hollow near Kimpergill Hill about two thirds of a mile north of the village. The hollow lay between the hill and the fairly high ground of Lea Green and opened out to the south-west, enjoying a wide view over part of Wharfedale. It was just such a place as would trap any drifting snow and at an early stage of the storm the rising wind piled a drift across the hollow and completely buried the cottage to its chimney. The great depth of the drifts in and around Grassington kept all the population so busy that Dolly was completely forgotten.

Fortunately for Dolly she had a good stock of food by her, with some peat fuel in a little store that opened out of her house-place so that she was able to prepare herself a drink and a meal from time to time. After her first meal, it still being dark, Dolly returned to bed to wait for the morning. The night seemed interminable and more than once she got up, made a meal, sighed for the length and dreariness of the night, and passed a little more time in sleep. After two or three days of the storm someone in Grassington remembered the old woman and the situation of her cottage, and asked if there had been any news of her since the snow started. No-one remembered seeing her, and at once there was a stir and soon a party set out to see how she was.

It was only with some difficulty that they at last located her cottage under a large snow drift which was then more than roof high. A way was dug to the door, but only after repeated shouting was Dolly roused to open it to them. When told of her precarious position her only comment was said to be "Ah, barns, I thowt it nivver wod be morning: I been up monnye and monny a time but it nivver seemed as if it wod be leet, its' t'langest neet at ivver I spent i' mi life."

Some versions of the story say that soon after this experience Dolly was persuaded to move into a tiny cottage in Grassington; others that she stayed at Kimpergill until her death, but all agree that she was the last person to live out there in what the stories call "Old Grassington."

In the 1860's B.J. Harker, collecting material for his book *Rambles in Upper Wharfedale* (1869), says that "there were people living a few years ago who could tell strange tales about her." He suggested that the tales had been told only by a few of the older inhabitants, and as the exact location of her house had been entirely forgotten, they had probably gleaned the tales from their parents or other old folk in their youth.

He then gives the above story as told to him by a person who professed to be skilled in the local legends. This and other similar evidence inclined one to place the story at latest in the eighteenth century and possibly earlier, and it seemed that it might be worthwhile to hunt for traces of Dolly's house or for any factual basis on which the story might have been constructed.

A series of rough foundations noted many years earlier were visited again, and after the removal of a good deal of stone rubble it was clear that in a hollow behind Kimpergill Hill there were indeed the foundations of a small rectangular building which might possibly have been Dolly's cottage. These foundations were fully excavated with the owner's permission, and a longer story than that of Dolly was revealed, while Dolly herself seemed to be verified as an actual person.

The excavations revealed that the site consisted of a very primitive house with a one room outbuilding, the structure of the whole suggesting a very early date, probably medieval. The house was a building thirteen feet by nine feet inside with walls that were on an average four feet thick. The floor was the bare limestone with all the joints and clints and the irregularities always seen on a limestone pavement.

Many of the holes and hollows in the rock surface were roughly levelled with bits of sandstone flags and when covered with rushes or bracken, it would make a serviceable though cold flooring. The walls were peculiar in their construction. Many large limestone boulders, some of them four feet or more in length and three or four feet wide, were set up on edge in two rows and the space between packed in with smaller stones, though many of the filling stones were as large as most stones which are used today in building.

Parts of the walls were made with equally large slabs laid horizontally and placed as in dry walling. These massive four foot walls were carried up about four feet high. On the front and on one side, the builders of an enclosure wall which passes within a few yards, and which was built in 1790 or the years just after, had robbed the cottage of many of the intermediate sized stones, but had left the larger ones on edge, and rejected the ones which were too big to handle.

A doorway on the south side is formed by two rough limestone jambs, blocks five feet long and about the same high and eighteen inches thick, set on edge and two feet six inches apart. The building to the east of the house was built in the same way, but with more small stone in the walls, and the walls were not bonded into the first one as part of the same structure, but were a little newer.

As we enter the doorway of the cottage there is a small wall or screen sticking out from the west wall and behind this the fireplace is made by a proper stone "hob". The firestone or hearthstone is of coarse grit, nine inches thick and about two feet square, laid on smaller stones which raise it about a foot above the rock floor. Behind it there is another grit stone, a "backstone" set on edge vertically to keep the fire from the back wall.

Around the hearth there was a good deal of peat ash as well as a few ashes from a very poor local coal and some wood ash, along with a fair amount of broken pottery and other objects. In the back wall of the room there was a roughly formed cupboard made between some of the larger stones, with a bit of flagstone for lining.

The articles found during the excavations formed a very mixed bag. In one corner near the fireplace, there were a lot of pieces of barytes and other spar, with pieces of lead ore all from the lead veins which cross Lea Green, a quarter of a mile from the house. The many fragments of iron included a very fine sickle of an early type, some ox-shoes, a few hand forged nails which can be matched by some found in the excavations at Kirkstall Abbey, and parts of the iron strapping that had bound together a wooden bucket and a smaller wooden vessel.

There was part of a bronze spur and a very fine pewter spoon. The pottery is easily recognised as belonging to three distinct groups: a small number of sherds of Cistercian ware which may be fifteenth or sixteenth century; some coarser ware, parts of bowls and dishes of sixteenth or seventeenth century date, and a large number of fragments that fitted together and made two decorated plates.

The plates are of a red pottery decorated in patterns made with "slip". This is a very fine white clay mixed very thin, then put on to the red pot exactly as one puts the decoration on an iced cake, though the slip is poured from a container like a small teapot rather than being squeezed from a bag. These slip ware plates will date from the early seventeenth century and are an exceptionally interesting pair.

Without cataloguing all the many finds, there have been sufficient mentioned to justify a reconstruction of the story of the house, and to give material for some sound guesses about its occupants. From the structure of the building a fifteenth century date would not be at all too early for its building, so we first suggest that it was built here in that period, away from the village and out in the edge of the wastes. The only occupations to bring a man out here would be thatching or mining, and we know from their account books that the monks of Fountains Abbey were, about the year 1450 to 1460, buying parcels of lead ore from William Cokeson, at Grassington.

Now it is not too much to guess that this was William Cokeson's house, near the mines which were then being worked, and that the ore and spar near the fireplace were the traces of his store, which had often waited there for the monastic buyer. The sickle and spoon with the earliest pottery would belong to William Cokeson, or his son or whoever followed him in the next fifty years or so.

After William's death, the house may even have been empty, or occupied by another miner or shepherd. We know from the pottery that it was used again soon after the dissolution of the monasteries. In the seventeenth century Grassington was becoming an important place, the mines had extended on to the moor in 1603; and population was increasing, and stone houses were being built to replace the timber ones. Is it unlikely that this old house was left, its family moving into a newer house in Grassington.

Our next recognisable occupant is probably Dolly Gill. The stories of her and of her red cloak all emphasise her living by herself in this out of the way place, and suggest at once that she was probably a "wise-woman" or she might even have been called a witch. Her very poor house with its low thatched roof, snuggling down in a quiet rocky hollow amid old mines, the banks of prehistoric fields and near the large burial mounds of forgotten peoples, would be exactly right for such a person. Possessing little and living poorly, she still kept either for ornament or for some professional or sentimental reason, her two elaborate dishes of slip ware, with their fine and striking patterns.

We need to restrain the imagination now or else leave it to the playwright to reconstruct some of the weird scenes this house must have witnessed between Dolly and her scared and lonely visitors. Of her end we know nothing, nor of her burial. After her death the thatched roof soon decayed; later the few timbers which had supported it were taken for fuel and the house gradually filled with stones and debris until at the end of the eighteenth century its walls were partly robbed to make the nearby boundary wall.

All that then remained of Dolly was the legend of her adventure in the great snowstorm, of her red cloak, and of her association with an "old Grassington" whose very location was forgotten.

This story is not too fanciful. The pottery and the other articles excavated, and the house now cleaned out and well displayed, fill in even more detail than has been given. The work of the spade has thus dug up a story extending over the centuries, and allowed local legends, and some references in the nearly forgotten account books of the bursar of Fountains Abbey, to fall into place as part of a human story, no portion of which has survived in written history.

None the less, Dolly Gill now takes her place as a real personage, and the place of her dwelling can now be seen and admired.

(November 1952)

FORESTS OF THE DALES

Pendle Forest, Bowland Forest, Forest of Knaresborough, Langstrothdale Chase, Barden Chase, New Forest (Arkengarthdale), and many other such names often applying to areas that are today mainly notable by their sparcity of woods and trees, are spread over the whole of the Dales area, and raise a query in the mind of the person who encounters them on the map. Do these names really record ancient forests long since denuded of their trees, or do they denote something different from the popular idea of a forest?

During most of prehistoric times the Dales area was covered by forest in the popular sense, covering the hills to far greater heights than the present tree line. Ash, sycamore, elm, hazel and thorn made the backbone of the forests on the limestone areas, mixed oak woods were common on the grits. In a few places of stiff clayey soil, oak and hornbeam were the main trees, and it is likely that the magnificent hornbeams that are so common in Bowland today are remnants of such a forest assemblage in times long past. A little clearing of the forests had been accomplished by Neolithic and Bronze Age man, largely confined to small and isolated areas, cleared primarily to obtain better pasture and shelter for cattle rearing, but in the main they were still almost untouched when the Angles, Danes and Norse settled the villages we still occupy.

The village nucleus consisted of tofts and crofts – small enclosures with a cottage or hovel upon them – with its surrounding zone of small fields and occasional pastures. Outside this small settlement and dividing it from any neighbours was the waste, much of it well wooded. A large proportion of village names indicate woodland clearings – "thwaite" and the terminal "ley" (leah) being common examples. With the Norman Conquest all land was regarded as the property of the Crown and its use and occupation was granted out by the king to tenants-in-chief. Game and other property in the waste was reserved to the Crown or to the lord of the manor, and was strictly preserved. Where a large area of waste was reserved for game and hunting it was called a *forest* and this is the origin of most of our Pennine "forest" names. Canute is credited with issuing a Constitution of Forests in 1016 A.D., but modern research inclines strongly to the view that this character is a Norman forgery perpetrated by the lawyers of the time as a means of imposing the Norman forest laws upon the English under a title that would be more acceptable to them.

The term "forest" implies "outlying land" (foras) of little or no value except for game. Manwood in his classic "Lawes of the Forest" (1598) defines a forest as "a certain territorie of woody grounds and fruitful pastures, priviledged for wild beasts and foules of the forest, chase and warren, to rest and abide in, in the safe protection of the king, for his princely delight and pleasure – It is necessary there should be woods in every Forest, both to shelter, and at times to feed the Deer." A Forest always belonged to the king, but frequently the king granted his game and hunting rights to a subject, when the area so granted became a *chase*, e.g. Langstrothdale Chase. Leave was sometimes given to enclose a smaller area with fence or paling and to have sole right to game within that area – such an enclosure was a *park* and originated only in the licence to impark. Scale Park above Kettlewell was enclosed by licence granted to the Earl of Westmorland, in 1409, and was limited to 300 acres. Old Park and New Park, Skipton, are two others of the many Parks created by similar licence.

By the earliest Forest laws, forests were placed under a special jurisdiction of four senior thegns, with four lesser thegns holding junior authority under them, and two Tinemen were appointed to each individual forest. As the forests included the villages and hamlets within their area, often with a numerous total population, the common rights that these people would have enjoyed in a free village were usually secured to them within the forest. Other rights were added theoretically as a recompense for damage done by deer and other game, with the result that within the forest there was constant conflict of royal prerogative and the people's common rights.

To deal with the endless questions that could arise, and to preserve the forests, special officers were from time to time appointed. In the time of Henry II, 1184 A.D. the forests of England were divided into two jurisdictions, north and south of the Trent, and in each of the two areas a circuit of judges was established, called an Eyre of the Forest and consisting of four judges. The Justices of Eyre tried all serious cases, particularly offences against the person, but less serious cases could be dealt with by two other courts more local in character. The *Woodmote*, or Court of Attachment, or Forty Days Court, was held in the forest every forty days and was a court of preliminary inquiry from which offenders would be passed on to the second court, the *Swainmote* or Court of Freeholders. Forest officials (verderers) were the judges and twelve Swains or freeholders of the forest were the jury. They could order conviction and fine in all petty cases, but more serious cases were sent by them to the Justices in Eyre.

The offences tried at these various courts were distinguished under three heads – besides the offence against the person, were those of Vert and Venison; Vert was any offence which damaged trees, undergrowth or turf within the forest, and Venison was an offence against the game. Vert had three main varieties: *Purpresture* being an offence by trespass or enclosure, *Waste* being the clearing of cover by removal of brushwood, or saplings, or cutting trees without permission, and *Assart*, the clearing of ground and digging roots to make cultivated ground within the forest bounds. Purpresture was sometimes defined as making buildings, erecting fences or hedges or digging ditches without licence. Waste would include the act of a freeholder felling trees even in his own ground, without the granted permission of the forest officers. In other words, the inhabitants of a forest had to regulate all their activities so as to preserve the forest and the game within it, and for this purpose had to accept certain disabilities, including damage to crops by the game. In return for this they had privileges of pasture for pigs at certain times of the year, and turf and wood for fuel. In 1225, A.D. *Charta de Foresta* added to these the right of a freeman to have honey from the wild bees that might hive within his woods, while its greatest concession was that "no man from henceforth shall lose neither life nor member for killing our Deer."

The officers of the forest were many, the chief office being that of Keeper or Warden, usually a person of very high rank in the peerage. Verderers were officers who attended the forest courts. Foresters, usually four in number, were appointed by letters patent or by purchase of the office from the king, to look after game and timber. Each person owning woodland within the area of a forest could appoint a Woodward (a common personal surname in forest areas) to oversee his own timber. Regarders and adgisters were charged with making a regular survey of the forest, reporting on encroachments, hedges and ditches, etc., and with control of the pasturage of cattle and pigs.

The forests established soon after the Norman Conquest were added to by John, so that most of the country came under forest law. One clause of Magna Charta in 1215 A.D. disafforested all areas made forest during the reign of John, and a final Act of 1640 A.D. was for the Limitation of Forests, and cancelled the application of forest laws to areas and took away the royal power of granting and afforesting any new areas.

So much for the judicial side of the true forests, which to explain fully would need more than one article.

There are in the mid-Pennines many areas which from Conquest times at least have had "shire" names and most of which contain large "forest" areas – Blackburn*shire*, Richmond*shire*, Borge*shire* (Claro wapentake), Hallam*shire*, etc., and the same applies in Durham and Northumberland, Hexham*shire*, Bedlington*shire* and so on. These "shires" are definitely distinct from and less than the county-shires and are seen from the Domesday Survey to have originated as the dependent areas of the largest Saxon overlords. Within each of the pre-Conquest shires, were included many vills and townships (mostly called, though incorrectly, manors, in the Domesday record) legally dependent upon their overlord but in fact independent to the extent that the labour of each vill was mainly occupied by the cultivation of its own land and was not diverted to work upon the lord's demesne. Labour services were lighter than in the true manor and the chief services due were, besides the upkeep of the lord's house and fences, the payment in kind, corn and cattle, for his household use and the entertainment of the lord and his retinue on hunting and other progresses. Rents in money were mainly "pannage and cornage" for the depasturing of pigs and cattle on the waste.

The *shires* were areas of sparse settlement with wide stretches of moorland or upland wooded pasture on which the vills had their rights of common, turbary and the like, and over which the lord at the same time had his rights of game and residual fruits of the waste. This picture fits very closely to the structure of the forest areas in Yorkshire and Lancashire, so close in fact that along with other evidence it seems safe to impute the origin of many of the forests to the Saxon "shire-moors". The full forest laws of the South and Midlands never ran in the North, but parts of them were grafted on to this older structure.

One essential feature of the mid-Pennine forests is the presence of groups of *vaccaries*, each of them being anything from one farm to a small hamlet in size, set in a clearing in the forest, and engaged mainly in the breeding of cattle and a few sheep, with little arable land. In Trawden Forest there were five vaccaries and a survey of 1323 gives their value –

> "They also say that there are v vaccaries of Trouden, one of which pays yearly xiij^{s}iiij^d and able to carry I bull and xij cows –"

The other three carried respectively, 1 bull and 24 cows, 16 cows and 16 cows. "and they say there is greater advantaged to the king to adgist these vaccaries by a suitable number of cows, then set them to farm..."

Bainbridge forests had eleven vaccaries, of which Burtersett and Appersett were the largest, and the other nine are now represented by isolated farms; New Forest and Arkelgarth had two vaccaries each; Pendle Forest and Rossendale Forest each had eleven vaccaries. The population of the vaccaries provided minor officers of the forest, and bred stock for the estates and farms of the overlord. They maintained the small clearings with meadow land and some pasture, the principal pasture being got in the more open glades in the woodland.

In the *chases* the place of the vaccary is taken by the "lodge" distinguished from it by no important feature except that less emphasis was laid upon cattle breeding. In Langstrothdale Chase there were seven "lodges", named in 1241 with names still easily recognised – Crey, Huberham, Yoghamethest, Risegile, Depedale, Beckersmote, and Uhtredestall. Like Bainbridge which was built after the Norman Conquest as the principal forest town for Wensleydale Forest, so Buckden was of post-Conquest origin as the manor of the Chase of Langstrothdale.

In Barden Chase the lodges had each a small area of meadow ground, with pannage of swine, pasture for cattle, and a small area to provide feeding for deer in winter; they are still known as isolated farms in most cases. In the 14th century the lodges were Drebley, Barden, Launde, Gamelswath, Holgill, Ungayne, Elsow and Crookrise, and Holden. In the valuation of the lodges and vaccaries, in addition to the value of meadow land, other rights are included, "turf graft" (digging peat), "on-shot" or "over-shot" of beasts (straying animals), "pannage" for pigs, sale of wood, and other smaller items.

One of the oldest forest areas includes that of Blackburn and Bowland. In 1090-1095 A.D. William Rufus allowed Count Roger of Poictou to grant to Robert de Lacy the Hundred of Blackburn, the Forest of Bowland and the manor of Slaidburn. The Forest of Blackburn was subdivided into four forests, Pendle, Trawden, Accrington and Rossendale, each with its officers. There was a master forester each for the forests of Blackburn and Bowland. For Bowland, the Woodmote and Swainmote was held twice yearly at Whitewell and other times in the Court room at Slaidburn, still existing in the Hark to Bounty Inn. The officers of Bowland Forest are listed in an early manuscript as a Bowbearer and Chief Steward. "The Steward holds yearly two Swainmotes, a Woodmote court, two Courts Leet and two Courts Baron, to which inhabitants of Bowland do suit and service, in which all such as felled anie wood without lycens, or killed anie deere, were fyned; also, all actions under 40s were tryed." Other officers of the forest were twelve keepers for the deer. The Parkers of Browsholme Hall were the hereditary Bowbearers of Bowland.

The Forest of Wensleydale, all the valley above Bainbridge and west of the River Bain and Mearbeck, was created in the time of Henry II. Ralph fitz Ranulph of Middleham was Warden with twelve foresters and two grassmen (constables). The service of the grassmen was to carry malefactors taken in the forest, to Richmond Castle for imprisonment. The village of Bainbridge was built as the chief lodge of the forest, and a *quo warranto* document of 1227 A.D. calls upon Ranulph son of Robert to answer Ranulph Earl of Chester and Lincoln by what warrant he made towns and raised edifices in the Earl's forest of Wensleydale. He answered that the town of Bainbridge was of the ancestors of the same Ranulph by service of keeping that forest so that they should have there 12 foresters each to have a house and 9 acres of ground ... etc. After the building of the grange and vill of Bainbridge in the time of Robert, the foresters were the following – Fynehorne, Horm, Astin, Walter Hunsbane,

Roger son of Robert, Roger Porcarius, Meldredus, William Nobill, Thorfin Calvecape, Hervicius Longus, Walter Wyclous, and the two grassmen were Richard Schorthose and Robert Scoryffe.

Various rights were from time to time granted in the forest by its lord, the Earl of Richmond, e.g., in 1145 A.D. Count Alan of Brittany and lord of Richmond, granted to the monks of Jervaulx Abbey the right to dig for ores of iron and lead within his forest of Wensleydale, and to take the flesh of deer that had been worried by wolves. Some early charters show that the forester was always one of the principal tenants of the Earl of Richmond, and that he paid a fee for the office, making his profits from the many perquisites.

The old custom of horn blowing is associated with many forests, arising in two ways. First, to guide travellers through the forest as night falls, a horn was blown at Bainbridge at 10 o'clock each evening between Holy Rood (September 27th) and Shrovetide. By ancient forest law, the king could give liberty to individuals passing through the forest to take a deer or other perquisites, but it was demanded so that there should be no possible suspicion of poaching or secrecy that such a person should blow a horn if the forester was not with him. The custom of blowing the horn as a sign of honesty and "open-dealing" while in the forest preserves soon became widespread and is familiar to all readers of forest romances. Passengers through the forests payed a toll, partly for privilege and partly for protection afforded by the forest officers, and in the time of Edward the third there is record that the tolls of the forest of Wensleydale are very much reduced amounting only to 40 shillings for the year, by reason of the poverty of those who travel. At the same time income from agistment, that is allowed pasturage, in the forest of Bainbridge (the names seem almost interchangeable) is £20 by reason of the poverty of the country and want of stock.

The forest of Knaresborough was created in the time of Henry I, and the Scriven family provided the master Forester until by marriage of a daughter the hereditary position passed into the family of Slingsby where it has remained ever since. The bounds of the forest are still well defined and are marked on most maps, and marked on the ground by ditches, boundary stones and other clear marks. For a long period, however, the foresters of Knaresborough claimed an extension of the rights over adjacent parts of Wharfedale which had been created forest by King John. This area is not well defined, but certainly extended to Bolton Priory and the bounds of Barden Chase. In 1204 King John made proclamation "Know that we have disaforested all the forest of Whervedale altogether from all things belonging to forests and foresters.." but in spite of this, the Constable of Knaresborough Castle and his foresters claimed "puture", that is food for his horses and men and foresters, and the control of animals, of wood cutting, and all other rights. The Abbot of Fountains who held land in Staynburn and Rigton, part of this old forest of Wharfedale, complained of the imposition of puture, and he and the Archbishop of York along with the Prior of Bolton gave evidence that this part of the valley had never been true forest. In spite of the disafforesting proclamation by John, these exactions continued for nearly a century.

The Abbot of Fountains had considerable grants from the Mowbrays of land in the forest of Nidderdale, but this was probably more correctly called a Chase, as is the general usage in most of their charters. In 1175 when the Grange of Dacre was granted to them nothing was retained by the Mowbrays except stag and hind, wild boar and roe, and birds of prey; their foresters were to have no power there nor were they to enter the land granted to Dacre Grange except for the custody of the wild beasts and birds. In a later grant the Abbot agreed not to make any new buildings in the forest area more than a hundred feet away from any existing building, though they might make new enclosures or closes in the forest, provided the fences and ditches were such that wild beasts could jump across and return. The shepherds and lodge keepers took oath before the chief forester that they would do no wrong to wild beasts or animals and birds. From the extent of grants and other documents it seems that the forest of Nidderdale included all the upper valley right to the head and came down to the limits of Dacre which it included.

In parts of the Blackburnshire Forests the Woodmote courts were faced with many and continued cases of purpresture, digging in the forest area. In Trawden Forest there were many visible outcrops of coal and the temptation to dig these and to sell the coal proved too great for many of the inhabitants, particularly in the fifteenth and sixteenth centuries when coal was coming into more general use.

To give more selections from the abundant documents relating to the forests would take up an unwarranted amount of room, so must be left to be dealt with in some other place. A question that most naturally comes to mind is that of the transition of these areas from forest to their present condition, the date and causes of that change and the method of its accomplishment. With the end of the high feudal baronage in the fifteenth century there was a marked decline in hunting, a decline that had started much earlier. Grants of assart in the forests had proved profitable and clearings provided a bigger return as pasture and meadow than as wood. The extension of villages and continued cutting of wood for building and fencing, for fuel and for charcoaling, along with the browsing of animals on the young herbage, all contributed to the decay. Leland in 1546 speaks with a tone of sadness of the state of many of the forests – of Knaresborough he says "The Forest from a Mile beneath Gnarresburgh upwards to very Bolton yn Craven is about 20 Miles yn Length: and yn Bredeth it is in sum Places an viij Miles. The principal Wood of the Forest is decayed." Thoresby says "I have heard of an old writing said to be preserved in the Parish Church of Knaresborough which obliged them to cut down as many trees yearly as to make a convenient passage for the wool carriers from Newcastle to Leeds; now it is so naked that there is not so much as one tree left for a way-mark."

In the sixteenth and seventeenth centuries there are numerous records of house and bridge building, where no suitable timber could be found in Yorkshire but had to be brought from the Midlands or further afield. Mines had been granted within the forests of Nidderdale, Bainbridge, Arkengarthdale and New Forest, and iron forges in the forest of Knaresborough at dates early in the fourteenth century, and with them all went the right to fell timber and take wood for charcoal. With lack of care the process of decay and spoliation was hastened and by the seventeenth century the forests, as woodland, had practically disappeared. In 1771 there was a little preparation in the forest of Knaresborough for some replanting, when a nursery of 20 acres of oaks was planted by order of Council, but this had little effect, and the enclosure of the forest in 1775 finally robbed the area of all forest character except the name.

In other forests, the effects of continued assarting to accommodate expanding population and the demand for more and more pasture had thinned down the forest to a few remnant woods and to hedgerow trees and shelter coppices, which today form most of the descendants of the original woodland.

The list of Pennine forests would be of great length, but the following can be mentioned as forests in the truer sense.

Forest of Blackburnshire –

Rossendale, Accrington, *Pendle* and *Trawden* Forests.

Forest of *Bowland.*

Forest of *Knaresborough.*

Forest of Wensleydale or Bainbridge.

Forest of Chase of Nidderdale.

Forest of Arkengarthdale.

New Forest.

Barden Chase, *Langstrothdale Chase,* Bishopdale Chase.

Of less documented status there are a few other areas which have from time to time been referred to as forests, or as having forest rights and law.

Masham Forest (Mashamshire).

Halifax. The forest area is indefinite, but the Gibbet Law includes presentation by a forest jury, etc.

Swaledale Forest – above Reeth.

Applegarth Forest – near Richmond.

Lune Forest – tributary to the Tees.

Stainmore Forest.

Of these, the names in italics remain permanently upon the maps of the Ordnance Survey.

(September/October 1945)

THE THORN TREE

The most familiar tree on the barer limestone uplands of Yorkshire is the stunted hawthorn, gnome-like in the fantastic attitudes adopted by its trunk and branches. Unconsciously, almost, it forms the inevitable ornament or relief to our remembered picture of clints or limestone scars. It would be hard to find any place devoid altogether of thorn bushes, except on the highest fells. It is a tree rich not only in the fantasy of its shapes, but rich also in legend and in popular estimation.

We all know it as the "May tree," and in that name we are perpetuating the custom of centuries. From a time "beyond the memory of man" the May Day sports of rural Britain have been the occasion for the welcoming and the use of the may flowers. In the time of Henry VIII, the citizens of London, on the eve of May Day, went to the woods of Highgate, Hampstead, Greenwich and other places to cut branches and to collect the flowering may for the decoration of their houses. The may made the garland for the top of the maypole and crowned the May Queen. In ancient Greece it was venerated as the emblem of hope, and in Rome its wood was always selected to make the torches carried in nuptial processions and at nuptial banquets. The flowering of the hawthorn or "white thorn" could be counted on for May Day, and its lovely fragrance and the generosity of its blossoming made a perfect setting for the real spring holiday. Before the reform of the calendar, May Day fell ten or eleven days later in the year than now, and long years of observation show that in our reformed dating the hawthorn is in flower, except in the most northerly parts, by the 11th or 12th of May.

In the early calendar, calculations were based upon a year of 365¼ days exactly, and this was wrong by nearly twelve minutes too much, so that in 129 days the calendar was wrong by one whole day. When the mistake was appreciated, the Pope (Gregory XIII) applied a correction in a new calendar, the Gregorian, or new-style dating.

In making this correction an attempt was made to bring the beginning of the year back into the same place in the solar year as it had been at the time of the Council of Nice in A.D. 325. To accomplish this, a proclamation was made throughout the Roman Catholic world that 5th October, 1582, was to be counted as 15th October, thus dropping the accumulated error of ten days. Britain did not adopt this new-style dating until 1752, after which time the calendar date and the true season's date of May Day, have been different; by the continued correction the old May Day by the season's date falls about 13th May of the calendar, by which time the hawthorn is generally in flower.

Among the many legends associated with hawthorn none is better known in this country than that of the Glastonbury thorn. It is said that Joseph of Arimathea and twelve companions came to Britain to preach the gospel. Weary with their journey they lay down to sleep on the Isle of Avalon,

Glastonbury, where Joseph struck his thorn staff firmly in the ground. When they awoke a miracle had happened, the staff had rooted and burst into flower, a sure and definite sign that this was the place where Joseph was intended to stay. Glastonbury was founded, the thorn tree continued to flourish and was known for many centuries; it was destroyed partly at, and partly later than the Reformation. In some countries the hawthorn is also regarded as the tree from which the crown of thorns of the Crucifixion was cut, and special virtues thus attach to it.

An Irish belief, that is also of occasional occurrence in the North of England, says that no-one will thrive after rooting out an old thorn tree.

In Yorkshire -*thorn* is a very common place-name element and this suggests that specimens of outstanding quality or number were a prominent feature of the landscape some thousand or more years ago when the names were being given. Thornborough, Thornbury, Thorncliffe, Thorn and Thornes, Thorner, Thorngate, Thornhill, Thornholme, Thornthorpe, Thornthwaite with, perhaps, the very curious Thorngumbald, come to mind as Yorkshire examples, while Thorntons are so numerous that many examples of them have to have a distinguishing suffix – Thornton-in-Craven, -le-Dale, -le-Beans, -le-Clay, -in-Lonsdale, -le-Street, and Thornton-on-the-Hills do not exhaust the list. As a compound name, -*thorn* is less common, but still can be found as in Skyrethorns, Brockthorns, Paythorne, etc.

This extensive occurrence surely gives us some justification for regarding the thorn, whether white- or black-thorn, and in some of its other varieties as well, as a real "Yorkshireman," an integral part of the truly Yorkshire scene. The compounds with -*thorn* have been made by Angle, Dane and Norseman with many medieval and later distinguishing suffixes, so that no age or racial group in Yorkshire's history can claim a monopoly – all alike have shared the respect and veneration paid to this humble tree.

(September 1947)

CRAFTS
AND INDUSTRY

Meeting of the Waters, Cowling

Dan Binns

BESOM MAKERS
OF THE DALES

In parts of the Yorkshire Dales some crafts still linger that have persisted for centuries, still pursued by a few people either as a full time job, or as an occasional spare time occupation. Dry stone walling, peat cutting, clogging and besom making are some of these crafts.

The use of the besom, the brush made of ling (heather stems) or birch twigs, has become very much restricted and usually the besom is found only in the farm yard, the cowshed or the garden , its place being taken in the house by the machine-made fibre brush. When all house floors were laid with stone flags and before carpets were anything but a rare luxury, the flags were kept sweet and clean by sprinkling them with sharp sand which, being ground under foot in the walkng to and fro across the floors, scoured the flags most efficiently and continuously. The sand was made by "braying" down coarse sandstones brought in from the moor, or was purchased ready-crushed from the itinerant sand and scouring stone man, who visited all outlying farms at regular intervals. Every few days (and in especially particular households, every day) the old sand was swept out and fresh sand sprinkled down. For such sweeping nothing was so efficient and hard wearing as the old-fashioned ling besom. In the cobbled yard, the shippon, and on the barn floor the besom was always in use.

A normal progression was for the new besom to start its life in the house, or on the haymow floor, being passed over when the newness wore off, to the shippon or to the yard. An old besom is still seen near some house doors, used for taking the dirt off heavy boots as one comes in from field or farm buildings.

The demand for besoms was sufficiently large and regular to maintain a few families of whole-time besom makers, who travelled the Dales with their wares, as well as sending regular consignments to the various markets and fairs. At the same time many small farmers made a few besoms as an odd-time winter occupation, both for their own use and for their neighbours. The craft in all cases follows the same technique with only minor personal variants, and has generally been handed down from father to son for several generations.

There are still a few men who recently made besoms for their own use and for sale, some of whom used tools and methods that had been handed down from their grandfathers or even earlier forebears. One such craftsman who until recently made an occasional besom for his own farm, had no knowledge of the time when his family, the Hudsons of Broadshaw, did not make them; his grandfather used to tell of the besom making done by *his* grandfather, who in turn could go back by oral tradition for still further generations. This man was a true figure of a Dalesman, over 80 years of age, active in mind and body and full of traditional lore and tales of the past, loving nothing better than a "crack" over old times.

The materials required for making a besom are threefold; ling (Calluna vulgaris) for the head; ash for the binding; ash, hazel or other wood for the handle or shank. The ling needs to be tall growing, fairly straight-stemmed, tough and pliable; such ling is looked for on soft wettish patches of the high moors, as that which grows on hard, dry ground is as a rule lower growing, "curly" stemmed and brittle and does not stand such hard wear. One besom maker was the tenant of an upland farm with its land rising to heather moors, the farm, like all others in this area, having certain common rights on the moors – right to cut peat for fuel, "sheep gates" or grazing rights, right to hew stone for building repairs, to take wood for certain purposes, and to pull ling for kindling and besoms.

Some besom makers who are not so fortunate as to be tenant or owner of a farm with moor rights, seek permission from a landlord to take what ling they need, usually paying in return a dozen or two new besoms each year. The whole moor is travelled regularly by the farmer-besom maker in the care of his sheep, and the quality of the ling year by year is closely noted and the soil on which it is growing, closely looked to. In March the selected ling is either "pulled" or cut, the former being the more general practice.

Selected ling "bobs" are pulled up by the roots and the soil beaten off against a stock made from the fork of a tree sawn off to give a roughly Y-shaped anvil, which is carried round and stuck in the ground where the ling is being pulled. Alternatively, the ling is cut with a short, toothed sickle – a bunch is grasped in the left hand, the sickle passed behind it as near the ground as possible, the ling forced back and the sickle pulled forward with a partly sawing motion. This is very hard work compared with the pulling and seems to have no special advantage.

The pulled ling is laid straight on the ground with roots all one way, until a small flat heap is made, then the same quantity is laid over it, with the roots the opposite way. The two lots are rolled and bound together with a withy or a bunch of sedges to make a bundle. This is of no fixed size, but is approximately a good double armful. It is still remembered in Wharfedale that on one occasion two men cut between them 80 bundles in a day; this is a record as it is usually reckoned that a cut of 25 or 30 bundles is a hard day's work.

The cut or pulled ling is carried down to the farm or besom "shop" and stored for drying. If properly selected and "got", good ling will keep for several years without deterioration and so the occasional maker may only pull ling every two or three years as his stock is depleted, or on occasions when the season's growth is very good. The ling needs to be kept dry and the usual place for storage is on the "baulks", the rough timbers that form a floor over the cow standings in the shippon. This is kept dry by the warmth of the cattle.

At a convenient time the woods are scoured for a supply of sticks for hafting the besoms and in this close scrutiny of the woods, sticks suitable for walking sticks, shepherds' crooks, and tool handles are noted and cut in due season. Nearly all the besom makers are small dealers in these by-products of the woods and the man whose work we are following was not only skilled in selecting and making walking sticks and crooks, but was also a skilled and cunning carver of spoons of infinite variety and fine artistic quality, and made almost any article for domestic use that can be contrived out of wood.

The ash and hazel sticks for hafts are put to dry and season on the baulks with the ling.

The final raw material requirement is an ash trunk from which to make "spells" for binding. This calls for a trunk anything from eight inches to twelve inches in diameter and with a length of six or seven feet reasonably free from knots. Such trunks are not common and the search for them and for straight hafts demands a good eye and considerable wood craft.

Having assembled the materials, the first job is to prepare the ash "spells" for binding. These are thin, uniform strips of ash, about three-eighths of an inch wide and as long as can be got from the trunk. The ash trunk, stripped of its bark and after a few weeks drying, is put to soak in water; it stands with one end in a water trough for a week or two and is then reversed and stood with the other end in the water for the same time.

Our friend the besom maker had a block of wood about eighteen inches in length, sawn off a bole perhaps twenty inches diameter – a good chopping log –and in the top surface he had chopped a wide, shallow groove in which the trunk can lie, not quite parallel with the ground. Seated with the log between the knees, one knee up with the lower leg vertical, and the right leg stretched out, out of the way, he takes the soaked ash trunk and lays the right-hand end on the groove of the chopping block, the trunk extending over the left knee and under the left arm. It is firmly grasped by the left hand while the right hand wields a hammer with which the end of the trunk on the block is well and rhythmically hammered. The trunk is slowly moved forward over the block until about half its length has been well hammered along a straight line parallel with its length. Two nicks are sometimes made about an inch apart, the whole length of the trunk, between which the first hammering is done. The trunk is reversed and hammered from the other end until the whole length has had its share.

The object of the hammering is to loosen the outermost annual ring of wood, to such an extent that the strip between the knife nicks will peel off. It is started at one end with a penknife, and eased along by further hammering. Once the first strip is taken off and a loose edge formed, the hammering is repeated along parallel lines until all the outer ring of wood has been torn off in strips. The process is then repeated time after time until all the rings that can be loosened have been taken off. The inner core of two or three inches diameter usually fails to respond to this treatment.

The long strips of ash so got are further split with a sharp knife into full length slivers of three eighths of an inch wide and up to a quarter of an inch thick. They are smoothed and reduced to a uniform thickness during odd minutes around the fire in winter evenings, and stored for use. A sharp penknife is the only tool used for this job; the right hand holds the knife blade steadily across the left knee, over the end of a spell; the left hand pulls the whole length of a spell slowly across the knee from right to left. The knife is actually used as an elementary spokeshave, smoothing the spell to the right thickness, and working most effectively in the hands of the right person. The knack of using the knife this way is very difficult to acquire.

Some besom makers never practised the art of spell cutting, but used split hazel wands when these were particularly abundant. The well known family of Ibbottson at Threshfield, always used split or "riven" hazel strips, but it was difficult to get them with sufficient length. An old dialect poem of some sixty years ago and now only preserved by oral tradition refers to two of the Ibbottson brothers and their sister, who all worked together at the besoms.

> "Old Jamie's makkin' besoms,
> An' Jackie's rivin' spells;
> Dinah's fotchin' watter
> Fra t'owd Spring Wells."

At the present time, wire is rapidly replacing ash and hazel spells as a binder, and is just as serviceable while the besom is new; when the besom wears short, it is the practice to cut off the lowest binding spell, and so secure another three inches length of besom, and in an old type besom three spells can be taken off in succession and the life much prolonged. This cannot be done with the wire bindings.

The tools required for the making up of besoms are few and simple, the "besom engine", a "needle", a brace and bit and a knife. The "engine" (and this is a universal name for the simple contrivance) consists of a wooden stock, made of heavy timber in the form of a four legged stool, or a heavy tree stool, carrying the "vice" and the "rest". The engine will be best explained by taking a particular example, remembering that others vary from it in small detail, each man having his engine made by a local blacksmith to suit his own taste.

The stock is made of two inches thick oak, eight inches wide and twenty-eight inches long. It is set on four stout legs, set in near the corners with sufficient outward splay to give stability. The "rest" is a simple support, about fifteen inches high, made of a straight piece of three-eighths inch round iron carrying a crescent of strip iron ten inches across, shaped like a crutch head, and set at right angles to the length of the stock, and four inches from the end.

At the middle of the length of the stock is the "vice". This is like a large pair of pincers made of iron strip, the jaws about six inches diameter across the curvature, and the hinge joint placed fifteen inches above the stock. One leg of the pincers is fixed into the stock, but the other is longer, about twenty-eight inches, and reaches almost to the ground. At the bottom it turns at right angles along the length of the stock and makes a very comfortable foot rest. The stock is nicked out so that this leg can swing in almost to the vertical position and close the pincer jaws to about four inches across. With the long leg and foot rest to the front, the rest first described is at the right-hand end of the stock. Some have a knee rest instead of a foot rest.

To make a besom, the first job is to sort the ling. It is sorted by two qualities; its coarseness, and its length. A separation is made into coarse hardwearing thickish-stemmed ling, for heavy duty yard brushes, and finer stemmed, more flexible and softer ling for house brushes. These are then sorted and cut to lengths between eighteen and twenty-four inches. A supply of the longest is laid out on the ground all stems set parallel and the same way, well chosen for straightness and even quality, to form a flat mat. Only experience will judge just the right amount. On these a smaller quantity of stems is laid next, an inch or two shorter, with the thinner ends of both sets coinciding. One old besom maker then places down the middle a thin handful of stems set the opposite way, with the root end to the bottom and the branching ends where the haft is to come. This he says always shows him the middle of the bundle, and is useful when hafting.

The composite "mat" of ling is then deftly rolled up, and under skilled hands the resulting bundle is entirely symmetrical, the reversed bit in the exact centre, with concentric rings of short and longer ling outside it. String or withy is placed round the bundle to hold it safe until it can be bound.

A tied bundle is picked up and placed in the engine with the bushy end resting on the "rest" and the "vice" grasping the stems about a foot from the end. Pressure with the foot, alternating with turning of the bundle soon makes a compact round bundle, and as soon as this is tight enough it is gripped in this position in the vice. The "needle" (sometimes called a "twizzel") is a piece of iron about ten or twelve inches long, with a cross piece or half circle bend at the top to serve as handle. The stem of the needle is half round and hollow like a joiner's gouge in section, with the hollow to the outside when held in the hand like a miniature umbrella. The blade or stem will be about half an inch across. This needle is thrust well into the bundle of ling, near the vice jaws, where one of the binders is to be made. The first thrust goes well into the middle of the bundle, and when the needle has reached its position and has been given a quarter rotation by means of the handle it opens a slot through which a prepared ash spell can be threaded. The needle is withdrawn and the bundle gripped hard with the vice whilst the spell is wound round the bundle carefully, then pulled as tight as possible. It is taken round a second complete turn, then begins to be "sewn in". The needle goes in to the bundle alongside the last turn, passes under the binder and emerges at the opposite side of it, at about one eighth circumference. The spell is threaded, pulled through and tightened, then crossed over and threaded in again in similar fashion.

In this way the third turn of the spell sews over and under the other two, and finally is taken deep into the middle of the bundle or turned at right angles up the bundle to bind in under the next binders. The tightness and neatness with which this binding is placed are amazing. Three sets of binders are made at about three inches apart, moving towards the haft. Three more are then put on but placed much nearer, an inch and a half or even an inch apart, and these come on to the part of the bundle where the shorter stemmed inner group fall short, and so help the besom head to taper nicely to the haft. Some makers put five binders, some six, seven, or in special cases even eight binders on the head.

All through this work the head is held in the vice, constantly being moved up, turned round, and shifted into a suitable position so that the treadle seems almost constantly at work moulding and compressing the bundle to shape.

The haft is next prepared, and the end that goes in the besom is flattened and a hole drilled through it at right angles to the flats. It is laid on the besom head in such a position that the hole will come between two of the broad spaced binders, if between second and third it will allow for one or two being cut to prolong the besom life. The end of the bundle is marked on the shaft with a slight nick, and then the shaft is hammered into the besom, down the centre reversed handful of ling, until it is in to the mark.

A quick probe with the needle verifies the position of the hole, and a prepared ash peg is then driven right through the head, passing through the hole. The stem ends against the haft are trimmed with a sharp knife, a few untidy ends at the other end cleaned up, and the besom is finished.

There is not a great deal of variation from the method just described. Some makers specialise in hard-wearing long life besoms, some in finer quality household types. Some use more binders than others, some fasten the haft with a nail instead of a peg, and some supply the heads without a shaft, to be shafted according to the fancy of the purchaser. A good besom head will wear well until two of the binders have been cut off and the besom rides on the end of the shaft when used, and if the shaft has been well used, it can then be taken out and used in a new head. The old besom head is broken up, and makes excellent kindling for the household fires, and so everything about it, if ash or hazel bound, is finally used up with no waste.

One special kind of besom that was occasionally made, used bell heather, the true Erica, called "silk ling". These besoms were light, and smaller than ordinary, mounted on a longer light haft, for the women to use in sweeping down the cobwebs from the granary and hay mow. On not many farms was such sweeping done at all regularly, and the making of these besoms was a very special art of one or two makers at the most.

For some purposes birch twigs are occasionally used instead of ling, but these are a rare type in the dales area, where ling is abundant and birch not so easily obtained.

For many years now, besom making in West Yorkshire has centred more or less around mid-Wharfedale, and it is there that a few besom makers remain, and their traditions are still alive. Best known of all the families concerned with this craft are the Ibbottsons of Threshfield, in the upper part of the valley. The first Ibbottsons to come to the area are said to have been moss troopers, who came from the Borders in the time of King James, and who made a living in this area by horse dealing and various allied jobs. In the middle of the seventeenth century they built a very attractive and typical dales house. Ling Hall, at the bottom of Threshfield village, against the stream, which like so many dales houses had house and barn (or laithe, to use a local word) under one continuous roof.

For generations the Ibbottsons were well known at all the northern fairs, wherever horses were shown or sold, always ready to deal in horses and ponies, and to sell besoms and other produce of the woods and countryside. Coming to recent generations, the grandfather of the present members of the family was known everywhere as Besom Jamie, his son who followed in the business being Jimmie Jamie. The besoms were made in the laithe adjoining the house, and some of the work done in a room of the house as well.

The produce of the family included all kinds of besoms, both ling and birch, birches for schools, walking sticks, shepherds' crooks, pea sticks and stakes for gardens, and holly. Besoms were carried by wagon to Skipton market each week, and large consignments were also carried to fairs in the north, Brough Hill, Askrigg, Long Preston, and others.

Besom Jamie bred some fine horses; among them one called Pigeon is still remembered as a great racer, winning races at all the horse fairs in the north. The Ibbottsons brought much of the ling they used from the moors around Simon Seat and Bolton Abbey, though another old maker in the same parish, Jos Story of Gams Bank, got his ling from Threshfield moor. This was always said to be much coarser and of less lasting quality.

At Skyreholm, near Barden, in the mid-valley, there have been several besom makers. Old Will Atkinson was a striking character, somewhat of a miser, living by himself. His ling was brought off the moors north of Bolton Abbey. He was followed in Skyreholm by Tom Lister, who until recently made besoms at Hough Mill, getting his ling on Barden Moor each March. He used ash binders for the most part, with occasionally a wire binder nearest the haft. Other families were located in the upper Washburn valley, around the now nearly abandoned village of West End, the Willises and Nelsons being well known for their besoms.

At Addingham, lower down the valley, the family of Roe worked up a good business, one of them going not long ago to the village of Draughton, and starting a besom shop there. He has been followed by Mr Petty, who still makes besoms for sale.

It is doubtful if besom makers were ever paid for the time and labour put into their craft, and it is certain no one could make a living from besoms alone, without the by-products, or the safe backing of a farm. The finished besom used to be sold for fourpence, and later the price was raised to sixpence. Just before the war they could be bought in market towns for one shilling. Remembering that the actual making takes nearly an hour, and then adding the time spent in searching for, selecting, and harvesting the raw materials, it is clear that this craft can never have been much more than a subsidiary seasonal or spare time occupation. Great pride was taken in the finish and balance of a besom, and this possibly explains the uneconomic return, much of the making was of the nature of a handicraft hobby, a traditional skill that was almost its own reward. Except in occasional outlying farms near the moorlands the craft is almost extinct, with no probability of its revival in this area as yet.

(July/August 1949)

PENNINE PEAT PITS

The difficulties with the supply of coal that have arisen during the last year have turned the thoughts of many Dalesmen to the supplies of peat to be found on most of our hills, and have prompted many questions about the extent of supplies, mode of getting, and value of peat as a fuel. Peat is worthy of some consideration in our Dales literature as one of our oldest native fuels, and one which in its getting still preserves many customary common rights that date back to the Anglo-Danish townships and their common byelaws.

The documented history of peat in the Dales area starts with the twelfth century when men were making gifts and grants of land to the newly established monasteries, either for the good of their own souls and those of their ancestors, or as a mortgage for the fitting out of expeditions to the Holy Land Crusades. In such grants, the rights of "turbary" – that is, the right to cut and use "turf" or peat as a fuel – where often given, and with it rights to pass over other peoples' land to and from the turbaries or peat-pits.

It will suffice to take examples from the chartularies of a few of the northern monasteries in illustration. In 1204 Roger de Lacy gave to Salley Abbey (near Clitheroe, but in Yorkshire) an acre of ground in Ratho (Lancashire) for a salt pit, and a sufficient supply of turf according to the judgement of his bailiffs. The turf was needed to burn under the "salt-pans", in which brine taken from the salt pits and from the sea was evaporated to make salt. In 1240 William of Coudray gave them another salt pan there, and granted them a "turbary" to dig peats "where they deemed best." Ten years later a grant of land was confirmed to them in Stainforth in Ribblesdale, and its position is described as being at the foot of the hill near the peat-road, and there is evidence that peat pits were already well opened out and working before this date. During the reign of Richard the First (1189–1199) they were given land and turbary rights in Gisburn township, and their land lay between the monk's turbary and the road from Rimmington to Gisburn Church. They also had peat pits in Ilkley, Oxton, and Litton. Bolton Priory account books include some references to peat, and in 1300 they have an item for the expenses of peat dug in Malham. They also had peat pits in the manor of Appletreewick and in others of their granges and manors. Fountains Abbey had numerous peat-getting rights, and among many others used peat at their smelt-mills at Brimham and at the place still called Smeltmill, in Nidderdale. The peat in this case was used along with charcoal for roasting the ore of lead in the first stages of smelting. In much later centuries, peat was the principal fuel used at many Dales smelt mills, the old peat houses at Old Gang and other mines in Swaledale being most impressive evidence of the large quantities used for this purpose.

The granting of rights of turbary to large monasteries was a cause of considerable unrest among the inhabitants of the townships concerned, as the local people feared that their peat supplies would soon be exhausted when cut on a wholesale fashion and carted away to the monastery. As a result of this suspicion there were riots and risings of many kinds and degrees. We get a clear picture of some of these in the proceedings of the Court of Chancery. About 1400 A.D. St. Leonard's Hospital, York, had cause to appeal to the Bishop of Winchester, as Chancellor of England, stating that they had in the township of Heslyngton, near York, a turbary which was their own possession and which they had enjoyed from time beyond memory, and which was shown to be theirs by their muniments and other records. Now, John Neuson and Richard Warthill "willfully and without leave of the Hospital cause turves to be dug in their turbary and proposed to continue so to do." The offenders had been called before the Earl of Westmoreland and Richard Norton, to show their right to cut turves in this way, but were not willing to say anything in justification of their actions. Further they continued from day to day not only to dig turves, but to make alliances and threats and disturbances. The Hospital asked the king to secure the issue of writs to bring them to justice, as the offenders were "so great in the country" that they could not be dealt with by common law. We do not know the result of this appeal.

In the case of Bridlington Priory in 1434, there is more detail. The monks of Bridlington had a turbary in Fraisthorpe, with 111 acres of moor, and there they had recently dug ("grove and gart grave" – good dialect from Old Norse "grafa" – to dig) and dried 409 cartfuls of turves and made 20 cartfuls of hay and thatch. On the 22nd day of June the vicar of Burton Agnes with others got together a mob of 60 persons and more, armed and arrayed in the manner of war and riot, and came to Fraisthorpe "and there the turves with sword and spades and other instruments hewed in pieces and case in pits and dikes so that neither good nor profit came therefrom." Also they menaced the tenants of the Prior so that they dared not go on to the moor.

Other pleas of a like kind show that in many of the peat areas, the monastic cutting on a large scale was bitterly resented, as would be any cutting on a commercial scale today that threatened the loss of local peat resources.

Without reciting the other abundant evidence of the monastic use of peat, we can pass to the domestic side of the matter. It is common in leases of houses and farms after the dissolution of the monasteries to have rights of turbary included and specified in the lease. An example from Airton will illustrate a common form; in 1625, Thomas Preston of Airton leased to Nicholas Walton, clerk, of Kirkby Malham, and Oliver Foster of Scosthropp, woollen weaver, several closes and strips of land in the common fields of Airton, which included the following. "Also a parcel being *turbary* and its freehold and soil in the south part of a close called Peedale.. also Dykeboddom to the south side of the turbary and free liberty to dig and grave turves and to lye and spread, set and dry turves upon the rest or north part of the close, and to have good and sufficient way through the adjoining close called Arnesayhause on Allermyre lane leading to Airton."

In many cases the turves were evidently cut from the small areas of swamp peat that had been formed in the hollows of the lowland areas, but in other Dales villages, the peats were got on the high moors. In Threapland several leases include clauses such as "A free way and passage up and down Cracoe Fell for fetching and carrying turves, peats, ling and stone with carts or carriages." (1590 A.D.) In Hebden many curious problems in arithmetic are set by the leases, as for example, in 1597, the lease of a farm in Hebden includes "two full parts of a part into twenty parts to be divided, of all ling and turbarye of the same pasture and also in the soil and commons waste and moores of Hebden Moor now not inclosed, all the said Hebden Moor into twenty six partes three partes of a parte the eighth parte of one parte and for five pence rent to be divided according to the rate of twenty shilling rent for one parte."

All this means that at the rent of 20/- per part, Hebden Moor was worth £26:17:11 and the turbary that was granted was a fortieth part of all the turf rights.

In the succeeding centuries there are abundant records of grants and claims of peat rights, and particularly in the lead mining districts, where experiments were constantly being made to use peat and peat-charcoal in the smelting works, with some small amount of success.

The getting of peat for fuel follows ancient custom and practice in most areas. Where the freeholders of a township have rights of turbary secured to them, individuals go on to the moor, select a working place and set out a turf-pit or peat-pit, both names being in common use. Year after year, this pit is enlarged and so long as it is worked each year it is regarded as the property of its owner. When the place has been selected, the top layer of sods and soil is stripped off, and put on one side, later to be filled into the hole made. The peat which lies just below the cover, and may be many feet deep is then cut into, and a drain or dyke made so as to drain away the water which usually saturates the peat. From this dyke head a "face" is started, that is, a long vertical section is opened out. The peat pieces or "turves" are cut from this, in most cases by taking off thin vertical slices, but occasionally by paring horizontally. The turves are cut either with a flat blade, like a garden spade, or a special turf-spade or "slane" or "slade", which is a flat bladed spade with a turned up section along one edge, standing at right angles to the blade. Peat is cut in thin bricks, varying in size, commonly about six inches by nine inches and three or four inches thick.

The cut turves are thrown out on the grass and laid out to harden. After two or three weeks they are set up in pairs on edge and leaning together, with one or two more leaned against them, so as to allow the wind to circulate among them. This is essential, as the conversion to a good fuel depends on the oxidation of much of the acid material composing them, and for this air is more necessary than warmth or sun. When dried and hard they are gathered up and piled in tall stacks, with a very open formation, as the peat improves in fuel value the more it is dried. Cutting never starts before the beginning of May, drying should be well on in July and August, and carting usually follows hay time or harvest. The peats are "housed" indoors when possible, or if they have to "winter-out", they are built into a close stack and thatched or roofed with larger peat slabs. As peat is much lighter and bulkier than coal, a good winter supply needs ten to twenty cartloads if no other fuel is to be used. The week-end is usually the best time to see the peat cutters at work, when, on many of the moors, the whole family is at work, father cutting, mother spreading out, and children doing their bit here and there as fancy leads them. Meals are taken and the whole day between morning and evening times for attending to stock, is made a hard working but happy picnic occasion.

In cutting a deep bog, at least two kinds of peat are found, brown, fibrous, easily dried stuff in the upper part, and below it, black, structureless, wet material that looks hopelessly unsuited for fuel. When properly dried, this deeper variety has a far higher fuel value than the fibrous stuff, but the drying takes great skill and careful stacking. In most townships it is not possible to take peat out of the township or give or sell it to people of other villages – the peat pits are part of the ancient commons of the village in which they occur.

During the last twenty years a great deal of attention has been given to the scientific study of peat, both as a fuel, and from the biological and geological points of view. From these studies it has been possible to ascertain the age of the various peats, and the composition of them, a composition which reveals the former extent of forests over most of our fells and accounts for the frequent occurrence of trees and tree roots in the peat. The varied content of the peats indicates considerable variations of climate during the last ten thousand years or so. These questions however are too lengthy for discussion in this present historical note.

(January 1944)

Bolton Abbey   John F. Greenwood

YORKSHIRE STONE

Today the proliferation of plastics, concrete, mechanical apparatus, of packaging materials of all kinds, coincident with the disappearance of the big household open fire and the unburnable nature of so many of the things we accumulate, has created a problem of rubbish disposal on a scale which is overwhelming the rural communities.

The Rural District Councils, with the best will in the world, and with the desire and necessity to find a tidy solution to their problem, now regard any old quarry as a providential hole in the ground which they can fill with their refuse, cover with soil and grass over.

The quarries which are disappearing are the field evidence of a past industry, once very widespread, of great variety, and a normal part of the economic life of the countryside. So long as stone has been a building material, quarries have been worked for the basic building stone and for roofing slates. Other quarries have been found for marble, ornamental stones, lime for the land and gravel for the roads.

When one looks at a picture and says, with an air of satisfaction, "that is a typical dales scene," the chances are high that the landscape will include more stone walls than hedges and that there will be a stone-built farm or a stone-built village, with stone roofs to the buildings. The scene may include rocky scars or even be of an individual feature like Malham Cove with its towering cliff of limestone.

We can be fairly certain that in the majority of "typical" scenes, stone in some form or other will be an important element. Stone and timber compete for the position of the most used and the earliest used raw material with which man in this area has secured safety and shelter for himself and his animals.

The rocky scars of all the dales have caves in which men sheltered at some time or other. In prehistoric times many caves were used and their primitive tools and ornaments, the bones of their animals or in some cases human bones revealed by excavation, have earned for the cave a place in scientific literature or in tradition.

Victoria Cave in Ribblesdale with many others around it; Dowkerbottom Cave and Navvy Noddle Hole in Wharfedale; Tom Tiddler's Cave in Nidderdale; Lady Algitha's Cave in Wensleydale, and so on, are only some of the many examples. Wherever the limestone scars are a part of the scene, they are known for the use made of them by men and women, mostly nameless, ranging from the first Azilian hunters of 10,000 years ago, through the fugitive Romano-British metal-working natives in the Roman occupation, to the Royalist Cavalier and Lady of the Castle of comparatively recent time.

The rich resources of stone, varied in character and widely distributed, have made the West Yorkshire folk natural stone-users through most of their history. A brick building is a rarity and comes as a visual shock, never assimilated, never settling down harmoniously into the scene as do the older stone buildings, many of which, with the tints of lichen on the walls and moss on the roof, appear more to have grown than to have been built.

A dales building, house or barn, demands a great variety of stones in its structure, rubble (rough lumps not shaped more than with a few hammer blows) often of limestone; squared rough grit for quoins; freestone (finer grit) for window and door openings; flags of slate or sandstone for the ground floor and thin, fine quality flags, usually called "grey slate" for the roof. Firestone, a hard, fire-resistant sandstone, was needed for the fireplace, oven and bakestone.

All these varieties of stone are present among the rocks of the fells and can generally be found locally, though each variety is found in one or two places where the quality is high and where the stone is sought for special purposes.

Building houses and barns has, however, been by no means the only usage. From prehistoric times the people ground corn by hand mill or quern, or from the Norman Conquest by the stones of a water mill. Millstones have given their name to the rock from which they were hewn.

The Millstone Grit, and the places from which querns were got, are remembered in place names such as Quernmore, Quernstangill, Quernhow, Whernside and so on. This last name is derived from the Old Norse *cweorn* – a hand mill or quern, and the *side* is Old English, a hillside, so we have the hill or hillside where querns were hewn.

These names are found in documents as early as 1202 and, as querns are common in the Iron Age settlements, their quarrying and making certainly extends back to the centuries before the Roman invasion. It had become a traditional practice when Norsemen came in the 10th century and gave the places their own name.

Stone and stone-getting have written their name widely over the Dales, and the maps can tell of uses now almost forgotten. There are more than 20 places which carry the distinguishing name, in some form or other, of Bakestone – in Old English *Beacstan*, a baking stone. An early (medieval) example is Bakestanberghe, "the bakestone hill"; later modifications are Backstean Gill, Backstone Beck, Baxton Fell, Baxongill, and so on, all in places where we can see the flaggy, fire-resistant rock outcropping.

There are old quarry names, Bakestaingraftes, Bacstayngrave (1340) and Baxton Delves (*graefen*, Old English, a quarry or pit, and *delf*, Old English, similarly a quarry or digging) but the number of grass-grown hollows along the outcrops of this quality of rock is a more convincing testimony to the very wide use made of it in past times.

Geologically the "bakestone" is a sandstone which will stand direct and prolonged contact with fire without splintering or breaking up. It must have occurred to some observant man in early ages that among the stones making his fireplace there were some, occasionally, which were not affected and which did not need a frequent replacement. In time such stones were connected, through popular experience, with particular places.

At a later time when names were being given, the "firestones" were christened, a name the geologists and miners perpetuate in the Firestone Sill in the North Pennines, and the more specific names like Bakestone Fell, to name the hill where they could be got.

Bakestones were used in two principal ways, as ovens built of firestone blocks and as large flags for oatcake making. The oven of the Middle Ages, and used as late as the 18th century, was a massive beehive-shaped structure at the side of the fireplace. It had a level floor and a domed top with a square doorway opening into it. It was usually about two feet or at most three feet in diameter and the same height.

A bakestone was heated by burning faggots inside it until the thick stone walls were at the right temperature; then the fire was raked out and the oven swept. Bread and dough cakes were put in with a long-handled shovel, or "peel," and the opening closed with an iron door. The bread then baked slowly as the stones gave up their heat and the oven cooled. Such ovens are a regular feature in the 17th century "inglenook" fireplaces of the Dales farmhouses.

In cottages a frequent feature, in the recess between the fireplace jamb and the outer wall, is a large table-like slab of firestone with a small individual fireplace under it. The top surface is ground smooth by a liberal use of sand and a rubbing stone. This slab is the true bakestone on which, when the fire underneath has brought it to the right heat, the oatcakes are baked.

In upper Ribblesdale there is a place on the river called Helwith Bridge, around which there is a cluster of quarries both old and new. The name Helwith is again Old Norse and refers to the ford with flat stones, and the quarries around this ancient ford are working flaggy rock called by the geologist Horton Flags, a name derived from the next village up the dale where they also occur.

It is a very hard and fine-grained blue rock of Silurian age, which, in parts, splits into slabs of great size but of thicknesses of only a few inches and as little as one inch. An early use of some of these flags was in the clapper bridges across local streams and these are still as sound as ever after many centuries of use. In Ribblesdale and some of the adjoining dales generations of housewives have been proud of the blue flag floors of kitchen and pantry.

Even wider afield than the floors the "Horton Flags" or the "Helwith Flags," as they are indifferently called, are to be seen in pantry shelves, in milkhouses and dairies. They are ideal for this use, as the flags can be got in varied lengths up to eight or 10 feet and of widths up to several feet.

Many old houses have shelves of this type with circular holes in which to seat the milk bowls for the rising of the cream, or rows of such shelves for maturing the cheeses in due season. Rougher flags, tall and narrow but thicker, make many gateposts, sometimes frame window openings, and have a variety of uses. Within a radius of many miles of Dales country, therefore, the flags are to be seen in use in and about almost any type of building.

Large rainwater storage tanks set beside or behind most farmhouses, handy reservoirs for soft water in a limestone country, were made of five large Helwith Flags. The base was grooved and the four slides slotted into the grooves. Two side slabs also had grooves into which the end slabs were fitted. The fit was so good that only a trace of mortar was added for final safety. The whole was tightened together with two long cross bolts made by the local blacksmith.

Besides these household tanks, which might be six feet by four or five feet wide and deep, the flags supplied many larger tan pit tanks and industrial vats. Countless thousands of gallons of "stone trough ales" have been brewed in part within the containing Helwith Flags.

These quarries around Helwith Bridge are still working, but today concrete has taken the place of the flags and the Helwith stone is broken down for concrete aggregates and road metal. The modest quarries of the 17th and 18th centuries are now seen alongside rapidly expanding, largely mechanised quarries where output is measured in terms of 100,000 tons or more each year.

Nevertheless the 20th century giants have their roots in the past and have grown out of the experience of past generations of quarrymen.

In most of the Yorkshire Pennines the Millstone Grit series forms the upper part or cap of the fells and few villages are far removed from a bed of grit. In Dales building, therefore, it was a common practice to open a small quarry on the waste of the moorland, at the lowest of the suitable grits, get the stone and trim it on the spot, then sledge it down the hillside to where it was wanted.

These little quarries served their purpose and then may not have been used again unless they had stone of a special quality when they might be worked for sale. Even then the work was usually intermittent, the farmer-quarryman working to fill orders and working on his farm between times.

In working the quarry the larger masses might be levered out by their joints on to the quarry floor, then split up this way. A row of narrow rectangular holes were pecked out with a sharp-pointed pick along the line to be split. When these were deep enough, steel edged wedges were tapped into them, perhaps three or four inches apart and gently hammered until they "bit." Then with a very special and rare skill the quarryman struck the wedges one after another, all along the line, with a heavy hammer.

The blows had to be such that every wedge tightened with just the same thrust, and only the fine ear and delicate muscles of the hammerman could judge this. Blows were repeated, keeping all the wedges equally tight, and the stone was left at the right point, to "work." Very soon it was split off at the line and the wedges released. These large splits were cut again and trimmed to size on the bank by the quarry mason or bank hand or banker.

The final shaping to a precise pattern was done by the mason on the building. Wedges were often lost and many have been found around the old quarries. Deep-cut sledge tracks can lead one to the little quarries, and the wedge slots tell of the early working.

A very important stone in the making of the house was the roofing slate. The thin, fine quality flags suitable for this use were not so common as the coarser grits, and the best were found among the series of the Yoredale rocks, which occur below the Millstone Grit. One or two horizons were specially good and, where these horizons were accessible, slates were quarried or even mined for a very long time, and carried far and wide over the Dales for the better quality of building.

Where oak was available, new timbers were cut out while the wood was green and amenable and in the course of centuries, with creaks and groans enough to account for all the ghosts on record, they have warped and settled to their present lovely curving shapes.

The weight of the rather thick stone slates, which were all that could be obtained on the Pennines, demanded a flatter roof pitch, as the slates have to rest on the roof more by their own weight than by any attachment, and the flatter roof pitch means heavier timber. So out of these varied factors has grown the peculiar sturdiness and fitness of our roofs, their pitch not rising above 35° or occasionally 40°.

When the roof is set up the walls carry the heavy rafters, usually at ten feet intervals, and on these are set the purlins, two on each side. In most roofs they run only from one rafter to the next. These are now sagged and bent in more than one direction. Spars lie across the purlins, their feet on the wall head and their ends meeting against the ridge tree, lying close set and parallel to the rafters.

Laths are fastened horizontally across the spars at intervals which vary with the size of the slates. The spars are usually split out of oak branches by simple quartering and are curved in lines which give an unusual beauty to the underside of the roof.

The slates are ranged in sizes and herein lies much of the charm of a roof— the gradation of the slates from eaves to ridge enhancing the perspective and giving life to the texture which nothing else could provide. When the laths are fixed, the slates are laid on, with an under-eaves course on the wall top to keep the wall dry. Slates up to a yard long are found in this course.

The size of the slate is measured from its fore-edge to the peg-hole near the top; a 27-inch slate is that length from edge to hole, and may be of any width. The under-eaves may thus be 36-inch slates, and when they are an inch-and-a-half or more thick they are no mean weight to get up a ladder and into position.

The under-eaves rest with their front edge about four inches or more overhanging the wall face and lie on the first lath, so that an oak peg driven through the hole will lie behind the lath and prevent any sliding of the slate. The next course must be longer than the under-eaves as they come to the same edge but go beyond the thickness of the wall and on to the second lath.

The third row of slates must be so placed that its forward edge overlaps the first row back edge by four inches, and also each slate is chosen for width so that the vertical joints come roughly over the middle of the slates of the row beneath.

Now with all this in mind and the regular diminution of the slates down to about 12-inches at the ridge, the spacing of the laths can be worked out when all the slates have been measured and sorted. Each row overlaps by four inches the row-but-one below it, and its joints overlie the middle of the slates in the next row beneath it.

Thus the laying of the roof provides an ever varying mathematical problem and the roof-layer is constantly calling to his man below for "a 23-inch slate to span 18 to 20 inches" or some other such combination. With a modern roof of thin tile, with all the tiles the same size or very few sizes, three-quarters of the skill and excitement are lost.

At the best slate quarries, it was possible to give the quarryman the area of the roof side, length and "height." He would deliver slates of varied sizes, sufficient to cover this roof in proper style. He had a large number of traditional sizes so that he could quarry on to stock, and he often charged by the area covered. In the 19th century it became more common to charge by the ton.

At the quarry the flaggy rock was usually got and stacked on edge on the quarry floor in large piles. These were left out to "weather," by which the action of frost and rain would show up or open their natural planes along which they would split. By this means the flag or slate finally used was in no danger of having thin sections split off it after laying.

There were slate quarries in Walden Head, on the ridge between Wharfedale and Wensleydale, which were being worked at the end of the 17th century by John Harrison and James Stackhouse, and in the fragmentary accounts which have survived it is seen that it was customary to give orders well in advance of the time when the slate was wanted.

In October, 1685, for instance, John Harrison sold Richard Wigglesworth twenty gaiges of slates, to be delivered "good and sufficient to the sight of any workman" by the 1st May next. Another order was given at the same time, to be ready and delivered in June "two years."

John Calvert with John Harrison agreed to lead several loads down from the Hard Raike (the quarry name) in Walden Head to Starbotton, a village in Wharfedale and to "lay it on this side of ye Milne bridge about John Simonsons or in some place where I may come to it not being troublesome to anyone." In an order for 20 gaiges they were to be paid on demand when 10 had been delivered.

These orders follow a general pattern which applied at most quarries – the stone was got, and by a specified date was delivered at some convenient place on a road. It was brought down from the quarry in sleds and then picked up by cart for carriage on a separate account to its destination.

The slates which occur between three limestones, the 5 yard, the 3 yard and the Underset, near Hawes, were known as the Lower and Upper Hawes flags, and these were of outstanding quality, famous for many years.

On Askrigg Moor the same stone was worked, and a quarry in it at Blackstone Edge was let to a partnership in 1774 with a condition that slate was to be sold in Askrigg before being offered to strangers. A quarry in High Straits Lane, Askrigg, and quarries at Carperby, also in Wensleydale, sent roofing slates and fine flags over a very wide area of the dales. In Dentdale, and around Muker and Keld in Swaledale, there are other slate quarries, and some in Coverdale, all of which had good names at various times.

The character of their slates vary and it is often possible to name, with a fair degree of certainty, a roof as being of Coverdale or of Hardraw slate and so on. The heavy demand on strong timber which slates made, and the arrival of the railways in the west of Yorkshire, caused a turn over to Welsh slate about the mid-19th century, and today it would be a difficult matter to find any quarry where slate in the Dales sense – a sandstone "slate" – could be bought.

(April 1971)

STORY OF THE LIMEKILN

An inconspicuous but persistent detail of the landscape throughout the Dales area and, in fact, over most of the Pennines, is the half-obliterated limekiln and the green tracks associated with it.

Not many structures can show such a uniformity of basic design combined with definite local characteristics and fashions in detail. In the limestone areas of the Dales it is often difficult to separate the limekiln from other elements of the scene; it nestles into the hillside, taking on the appearance of just another smaller, tumbled outcrop of limestone, partly disguised by the small quarry scar which is so often its companion.

Most commonly it draws attention to itself only by the dark opening of the drawing arch, appearing at a short distance like the mouth of a tunnel, with a rather massive and disproportioned supporting masonry surround.

Few people nowadays see the kiln as a live spot of fire with the glow of the ash door flashing across the valley, or the column of drifting steam and smoke rising above the kiln and lit up momentarily as the filling settles within. A few artists have found such a subject acceptable for their art, and scenes such as Turner's painting of the limekilns at Coalbrookdale or Girtin's kiln near Richmond are some of the rare depictions we have of this once common scene.

Pyne includes the limekiln and limeburners in his Microcosm, 1823, as the legitimate subject of one of his plates illustrating the everyday occupations of his time, and writers of the standing of Hardy and Dickens have found in the kilns and their surroundings all the elements of the spectacular in the vivid contrast between the glowing furnace within the shelter of the arch and the cold, darkness and wild weather outside.

One surprising thing, as soon as one begins to ask about a limekiln, is the paucity of information, even among country people, about the age of the kilns, about the methods of their use and about the people who used them.

All will readily agree that the kilns belong to past generations and some will hazard a guess about the way of lime-burning, but not many folk have any memory of their activity beyond, perhaps, the tradition that their father, or more likely their grandfather, used to fetch lime from such and such a kiln, sometimes from an amazing distance.

The lime was brought in carts or on pack ponies, or more often brought by regular lime-carriers. An old farmer in Wharfedale used to fetch lime from Greenhow Hill kilns, setting out soon after midnight with horse and cart to walk eight miles over rough ways to the kiln, load up and get back for his day's work on the farm. He was farming in the gritstone area near Bolton Abbey and thought and maintained that Greenhow lime suited his land better than any other.

Fifty and more years ago he was near the end of a long tradition, in which his father and grandfather at least had worked, liming sour land and bringing moorland "intake" into sweet pasture with the help of fresh lime and hard grazing.

As a building material for mortar, lime can claim an ancestry right back to Roman and possibly earlier times. The power of lime and sand to set to a strong cement with slow hardening was an early discovery, and the building of special places to make the lime was part of any planned building operation.

In this country there is abundant evidence available which shows that one of the first tasks of builders, civilian or monastic, was the preparation of a limekiln.

Although the term "kiln" is used in the documents of the thirteenth and fourteenth centuries, some of those early structures were unlike those whose remains are now so widely scattered over the Pennine hillsides.

Some of the early kilns were circular places, ten to fifteen feet diameter, walled round to three or four feet height. Inside this kiln a fire of brushwood was started and alternate layers of coal or turf and broken limestone were added.

When the kiln was well alight, and the fuel and stone filled to the top of the wall, the piling of alternate layers of fuel and stone was continued in a conical pile; then the whole was covered in with sods to regulate the burning. Once completed the kiln was left to burn itself out, when the collapsed mass of burned stone and ashes was led out.

It is clear that only a dirty lime could be produced in this way, but as ashes were often used in making the lime mortar, the admixture of some from the kiln was no real disadvantage.

A kiln of this early type, whose date is fixed with certainty, was recently excavated at Ogmore Castle, Glamorgan, and several others associated with early castles have also been described. The one at Ogmore is a circular structure, rather small but preserving many details with great clarity.

The wall of it is a dry stone wall six feet thick, and enclosing a circular space 5ft. 8in. diameter at the ground, 6ft. 8in. diameter at the top of the walls which are now only 2ft. 9in. high. This shows that when complete the inside was a tapered bowl, probably of much greater depth.

On opposite sides at the base there are wind tunnels, 4ft. 5in. wide at the outside, and narrowing to 1ft. 3in. at the inside of the kiln. They are 1ft. 9in. high and corbelled over with large flagstones. The floor of the kiln when excavated was still covered with fragments of coal and lime, and there was a layer of coal ashes and lime outside, to eighteen inches thick.

The kiln is dated to the late thirteenth century by the intrusion on to it of a fourteenth century building, in the building of which the top part of the kiln has been removed.*

The excavators of this kiln make comparisons with many other similar examples, and conclude that it is of the normal pattern used in that period. Kilns of this small type and pattern remained in use to the end of the sixteenth century.

George Owen in 1595 described the Pembrokeshire limekilns as follows:-

> After the limestone has been broken into small pieces it is put into a kill made of wall sixe foote heighe foure or five foote broade at the bryme but growing narower to the bottom, havinge two lope holes in the bottom which they call the kill eyes; in this kill first is made a fier of Coales or rather Culme which is but the dust of the coales which is laid on the bottom of the kill, and some few sticks of wood to kindle the fier . .

The most abundant mention of limekilns is in the State Papers for the thirteenth and fourteenth centuries, when repairs and alterations were being

---

* Craster, O.E. A medieval limekiln at Ogmore Castle, Glamorgan. *Arch. Cambrensis.* CI. 1951. 72—76.

The Old Lime Kiln   Margaret Hilton

made at the Tower, London, and at many towns and castles under the King's orders.

It is common to find entries in the Liberate Rolls and Fabric Rools, mostly in the form of an order to a sheriff or constable to have a kiln made for a particular building job. Examples of these entries are the following:-

> 1228, April 24. To the Sheriff of Oxford. Contrabreve to cause a limekiln for the works of Oxford Castle to be made where most convenient, out of the brushwood that the king has ordered H. de Neville to cause the sheriff to have in a suitable place near Oxford for this purpose. (Cal. Liberate Rolls 12 Hen. III.)

The confirmation of this order in 1229 apportions twenty-six acres of timber for the use of two kilns, one for work at the castle and the other for work on the city walls.

> 1228, May. The Sheriff of York was "to cause two kilns for making lime to be made in order to enclose the bailey of Pickering Castle."

Most of these early accounts are concerned with the King's castles and city walls at Oxford, Windsor, Winchester, Rockingham and, of course, the Tower of London. Usually they include some details of the cost or the capacity of the kiln, and these give some clue to the size.

In 1229 a kiln at Winchester Castle cost 100 shillings, while in 1240 £10 was ordered to pay for the collection of materials needed for building a kiln for the repair of Rockingham Castle. "Computate to Robert de Catteshale, constable of Lincoln, 20 marks expended in making a limekiln for the works at Lincoln Castle by the king's order" (Cal. Liberate Rolls. 13 Hen. III).

The size of these kilns varied considerably and was often specified by the amount of lime to be made; e.g. . . . "to cause to be made without delay a limekiln containing at least 2,000 loads of lime, for the works of the Tower of London"; and again ". . cause to be delivered to John son of Andrew £20 from the issues of the forest of Windsor to make a limekiln for 1,000 loads of lime in that forest for the works of the Castle."

Another order gives the Constable of the Tower "40 marks to pay for 600 pieces of wood that he bought to make limekilns for the works of the Tower of London." In 1239 there is an order "to cause to be carried to London 1,000 quarters of lime for the works of the Tower of London and not to cause the lime to be slaked before it arrives."

Such entries are numerous in the thirteenth and fourteenth centuries in the official documents, and a few examples from private documents of the same period show a similar arrangement.

In the contract for the rebuilding of Catterick Church, in 1412, Dame Katharyn Burgh and her son William are to find the lime and sand for mortar for the use of the contractor, and this would involve building a kiln at some convenient place.

Many of the monastic houses had a lime kiln of their own used occasionally for repair work. The charters of Fountains Abbey include several references to limekilns, and their accounts show that one was maintained at Kilnsey for lime for plasterers and masons repairing the various buildings in Upper Wharfedale and on Malham Moor. In 1298 Bolton Priory accounts include the sum of seventeen shillings spent on coal for the use of their limekiln.

In some of the mentions of a kiln, the reference is to making a pit for a kiln and for setting stone round the kiln, though by the beginning of the fifteenth century the nature of the references changes and a built-up structure is more often indicated, as at York where 3,300 bricks and 33 loads of clay were ordered for making a kiln.

The limekilns so far mentioned have all been connected with building, and most of them were constructed for the demands of a particular job and might rarely be used again, even if they were a more or less permanent structure.

The greatest change in the use of limekilns came about in the sixteenth century, when the value of lime as a manure, particularly in the improvement of sour or poor land, was discovered. The books on agriculture written then and in the seventeenth century speak of the value of lime.

Fitzherbert, in his treatise on Surveying, 1546, places marl, lime and dung together as the best manures for the general improvement of poor land.

Owen, in 1603, says that in Pembroke the farmers have burned lime in primitive kilns during the last thirty or forty years and have found that it was most efficient when placed hot in small heaps and left to slake in the weather.

By 1639 Gabriel Plattes and, about the same time, Gervaise Markham, can both say that the process of lime burning is now so well known and widely practised that it needs no detailed description. Besides being used for land improvement it is now mentioned as a good manure or preparation for arable land before a long series of corn crops.

It is about the middle of the seventeenth century that limekilns begin to take their place and be valued as property and even itemised in wills. One of the earliest in the Dales occurs in the will of Henry Holmes, of Hebden, who in 1621 leaves among his farming assets "one lyme kilne and turves, 12s."

A very good description of the making and use of lime is given by Mortimer in 1707, and part of it is worth reproduction:

> Lime is commonly made of Chalk or of any sort of Stone that is not sandy or very cold, as Freestone etc. All sorts of soft stone, especially a grey dirty coloured stone that if you break it will yield a white powder, and all sorts of Marbles, Alabaster, Slate, Oyster and all sorts of Sea shell .. the harder the Chalk or the Stones are the better is the Lime; only they require more fire to burn them: Both sorts may be burned with Wood, Coals, Turf, or Fern which makes a very hot fire.
>
> The Kilns used for Chalk or Stone they commonly make in a great pit that is either round or square according as they have convenience, and big according to the quantity they burn, which they make wide at the top and narrow by degrees, as they come nearer to the Bottom; The inside of the Pit they line round about with a Wall built of Lime-Stone; at the Out-side near the Bottom, they have a hole or door by which they take out the Ashes, and above that some have an Irongrate, which cometh close to the Wall roundabout; but others arch over it with large pieces of Stone or Chalk; and upon this they lay a Layer of Stone, or of what else they burn in the Kiln, and upon that a Layer of Wood or Coals etc. which they repeat till the Kiln is full; only they observe that the outermost layer be always of Wood or Coals, or what they burn their Lime with, and not of what they make their Lime, to which they give Fire at the hole underneath.
>
> Chalk is commony burnt in twenty four Hours but Stone often takes up sixty Hours; Ten Bushels of Sea-Coal or a Hundred of Faggots three Foot long will burn forty Bushels of Chalk and forty Bushels of Chalk will yield thirty Bushels of unslaked Lime .. But the Stone Lime is much the best for Land and indeed for all other Uses; which in many places they carry out upon the Land, and lay in heaps, allowing a Bushel to a Pole-square, or hundred and sixty

Bushels to an acre, which they cover with Earth, letting of the Heaps lie 'till the rain slacks it, and then they spread it.

But they reckon that if it is carried out upon the Land hot from the Kiln, that 'tis best . . .*

Many leases of farm land in the eighteenth century include clauses enforcing the use of lime, and one from the Barnsley area is quite typical of a very large number:-

1722. Lease between John Spencer of Cannon Hall and Henry Wood, on one part—Richard Robinson of Dodsworth on the other, of closes of land near Keresforth Hall, parish of Barnsley . . . and further also shall and will at his and their own proper costs and charges sett bestow and imploy sixteen horse loads of well burned unfallen lime or else sixteen wain loads of good and sufficient dung or manure upon every ordinary Days work with a plow by vulgar estimation and also the like proportionably upon more or less quantity of ground . . . which shall be plowed graved digged or sown with corn or grain at any time during the said term and shall not sow reap or take above three crops of the same ground during the said term (except only one crop of peas) for once so liming . . .

Many travellers in the latter half of the eighteenth century noted the increasing use of lime, and Arthur Young has many comments to make upon it.†

In 1770 he says, "Lime throughout most parts of the North is what they principally depend on, the benefit they urge to be great, and considering they use only *stone* lime, it doubtless is so. But from the intelligence I gained in many place, I have great reason to believe that this spirit of liming is not attended with the effects that many believe. The greatest use, that of forming a part in compost, is little attended to. Upon black moory soils the use is exceedingly great, much more so than on any other land."

When he was near Belford, in Northumberland, he noted that "discoveries of coal led to the burning of lime for the purposes of agriculture, as a manure, in a much larger way than had been usual; and for this work three new lime kilns were erected, in a most substantial manner, and at great expence."

He frequently insists on this value of lime in the recovery of moorland, and in many places he commends the practice of "intaking" moorland by paring, burning and liming. This consists of taking up the top heathery sod with the plough or spade, drying and burning *in situ* for the benefit of the ash, then spreading liberally with fresh lime before ploughing and cropping.

Bray, in both Derbyshire and Yorkshire**, noticed limekilns with interest, and gives us a good word picture of those near Stony Middleton, which were later the subject of a drawing by Chantrey.

"Over the town is seen the smoak of the numerous kilns, used for burning the rocks into lime for manure by means of which the most barren of these hills are fertilized. The kilns are built at the foot of the rocks from which the stone is got to be burnt; they work only in the summer, except one which is constantly in burning lime for a smelting cupola here.

"It takes up two days to burn a kiln; the lime is drawn out at bottom, and sold for two pence a strike, or bushel. The men earn from eight to ten shillings a

---

* Mortimer, J. *The Whole Art of Husbandry or The Way of Managing and Improving Land.* 1st Edition 1707. Quote from 3rd ed. London, 1712. Chap. IV, p. 68.
** Bray, W. *A Tour into Derbyshire and Yorkshire.* 1783.
† Young, A. *A Six months Tour through the North of England.* Vol. IV, p. 482. 1770.

week. Small carts bring a load of slack (the small part of the pit coal) from about Sheffield and Chesterfield, and receive for it a load of lime.

"Three strike of lime are considered a load, and from forty to fifty loads are laid on an acre. Coals are sold here for sixpence the hundred weight."

At Buxton, Bray noted that "there are seven or eight kilns worked in the summer, which burn from 120 to 300 horse loads in two days, sold at 4d. or 4½d. the load. It is sometimes carried away in small carts which hold about four horse loads each. Five men join in taking a kiln and give £5 a year for it. They work at the mines in the winter." Later in his tour he saw kilns in Yorkshire, and at one point says, "The stone of the hills about Maum (Malham) is burnt into lime, of which six pecks, each containing 16 quarts, are delivered at the kiln mouth for 7d. It takes up a week in burning, and when it begins to be calcined, the lowest stratum is drawn out at the mouth, and more stone and coal put in at the top."

Other travellers, such as Hutton, noted kilns around Settle, and quotations could be multiplied, but all give much the same picture of lime primarily in demand for the moorland soils or as manure on the corn lands.

This great insistence on lime as of value in agriculture and in the recovery of moorland pasture led to two great developments. In the limestone areas of the Pennines large numbers of farmers and landowners built small kilns for the improvement of their own uplands, while on the flanks of the Pennines and the gritstone areas, a demand for lime was created which encouraged the building of larger kilns as a commercial adventure, producing lime for sale.

This larger group was also encouraged by the rapid extension of canals which crossed the coal-fields and which made a supply of poor quality coal easy to get. In the promotion of the Leeds and Liverpool Canal it was stressed that the canal would link the limestone areas of Craven with the coal-field around Leeds and Bradford, and that coal could travel to the limestone areas and lime could be brought back. As about four times as much stone as coal was used in lime burning, it was generally the case that the coal travelled to the lime.

One result of this arrangement is the large number of limekilns still to be seen, or only recently removed, from the banks of the canals. Between Skipton and Bradford there were large kilns at Farnhill, Kildwick, Keighley and Shipley, some of them still to be seen.

From these two branches of the growing industry three principal types of kiln were evolved – the pye kiln, the ordinary farm kiln, and the large commercial kiln which was often built and operated in groups of three or four or more.

The pye kiln in many ways is a survival of the earlier primitive kiln, while all the others are what are called "running kilns" which once lit up, the process of burning limestone can be maintained for an indefinite period. While our main interest is with the second group, the farm kiln, the others merit a brief description.

We are fortunate in having preserved for our use the detailed observations of John Farey, Mining Engineer, made during his survey of the agriculture of Derbyshire on the instructions of the Board of Agriculture, inspired by Arthur Young.

Farey had a passionate interest in mines and quarries and all processes connected with them and in everything by which the geology of natural products could be applied in everyday life. His observations fill the two large volumes of the *General View of the Agriculture of Derbyshire with observations on the means of its improvement,* London, 1813, and summarise many years of intimate work and knowledge of Derbyshire.

He was so inspired by the importance of lime in the improvement of land that he listed all the limekilns that were producing lime for sale (as well as some of the private ones) and where he noted anything of special interest he would include a description of the process or structure of the kiln, or detail of prices.

Thus we can turn to him for a clear view of the limekiln as it was in operation at the end of the eighteenth century.

Farey described a pye kiln in operation at Newhaven, Derbyshire, and his description can hardly be improved upon.

> In a Stone Pit, if on an eminence rather, and open to the West the better, for saving carriage of the Lime, and procuring more draught of air, and if the Carts can come into the West side of the Pit, still better, as then the Pye is to be constructed upon the Eastern side of the Pit: those I saw were thus situated, and sixteen yards long, six yards wide at the top, three quarters of a yard wide at the bottom, and three yards deep, shaped much like a Boat with swelling ribs; the sides of the Pit having been roughly cut or quarried, to form the East side and the ends, and the West side formed with a rough wall of Limestones: three openings or door-ways being left in the length, in building this side-wall, which openings are built with Stones, previous to charging the Pye. Along the bottom of the Pye, a Channel is formed about half a yard wide, and as much deeper than it, like the keel of a Boat almost, and from this three similar channels branch, to pass under the three openings or door-ways; these are for admitting air, and lighting the Pye: whose previous preparation for charging as above, has cost Mr. G. from 60s. to 70s.
>
> Preparatory to charging the Pye, the Trenches above mentioned are covered over by dry branches of Wood, and Heath or Straw spread upon these to receive a floor or layer of Coals three inches thick, all over the bottom of the Pye: then six inches thick of Stone, broken rather small is spread open this; then another three inches of Coals, succeeded by a seven or eight inches layer of Stone, which may increase in size of pieces to the middle, where they may be pretty large, if set up edge-ways.
>
> In the above manner the alternate layers of Coals and of Stone are continued, the latter increasing in thickness to 14 feet above the bottom along the middle of the Kiln, and the last layer of Stone may be 14 inches thick, and should be pretty well broken, and the top layers should diminish above the walls, so as to form a regular surface, almost like a Boat five feet deep, turned bottom upwards. This surface is then to be covered with Sods, laid with the Grass inwards, and lapping close over each other, except along the ridge at top, to about six inches thick.
>
> Lighted Straw or dry Heath is then introduced to the middle of the Pye bottom, by means of the three side channels, and the Pye is left to burn for five days, if good Coals from the Wharf at Cromford are used, or ten days if the Thatch-marsh Coals are used: one or two days more are generally enough to cool the Lime, sufficient to begin drawing; which commences by backing the Carts against the side wall, and the men with Shovels throw the Lime into the Carts, until got some distance below the side-walls; the temporary Walls in the three openings or Door-ways are then removed and a Cart backed to each, enables the remainder to be readily drawn and loaded.
>
> Twenty five tons of Coals thus applied, make 80 three-horse Cart-loads of Lime, of about 30 heapt bushels each; a Pye, dressing about 20 acres, at the rate of 120 bushels per acre. Mr. G. did not seem to be aware, of any larger quantity of Lime being procurable from a Ton of Coals in this way, than by using Running-kilns, but considered the saving in time and expense as very considerable, with Pyes.

It is clear from the above description that the pye kiln could be made easily and cheaply in an old quarry scar, and could be used in fact to burn up land clearance stone, which could be accumulated gradually on the site.

The kiln is built to a particular capacity and used just the once, characteristics we have already noted in many of the early records of kilns.

The running kiln demands a more permanent structure and, in fact, only running kilns have been recognised among the many scores of kilns still to be traced in the Pennines.

The essence of the running kiln is the bowl-shaped burning chamber with a dominantly vertical arrangement. The commonest kiln about the beginning of the eighteenth century, little modified later, had a bowl diameter of something from eight to fourteen feet, though eight to ten feet was by far the commonest dimension.

For some six or eight feet down the bowl was cylindrical, then for another eight or more feet it tapered regularly to a bottom diameter of not more than three feet. In most cases a square structure was the massive containing and supporting surround of the bowl, though circular kilns were occasionally built.

At the bottom of the bowl a grate was inserted through which burnt lime and ashes could be raked out, though there was a good deal of variation in the detail of lime and ash hole. The approach to the bottom of the kiln was through arches in the enclosing structure.

The loading of the kiln was similar to that of the Pye. Alternate layers of coal and stone are filled in at the top, but as burnt stone accumulates in the lower part, it is raked out as lime, and more layers of stone and coal are added at the top. The process is continuous.

The advantages of hillside sites are obvious – it is usually so arranged that the limestone is quarried at top level and can be barrowed directly to the mouth of the kiln, while carts have access to the foot or drawing arch.

Such kilns are sited at the nearest point to the ground which will use the lime, if they are farm kilns, or as near as possible to good transport, road or canal, if they are commercial kilns.

Green tracks are to be found from many of the upland kilns, not only leading over the land to be recovered, but often leading away on to the more permanent pack-horse tracks, and there is no doubt that where there are such tracks the kiln was worked for more than local requirement, and farmers from round about or from other areas came here to buy lime.

Not every farm could have its own kiln, so it was inevitable that where good limestone was available there was an incentive to build a kiln for more prolonged usage, and no doubt, as Bray noted in Derbyshire, some of them were worked in the summer months by miners. This is a very reasonable occupation for the small miner, who often suffered considerable shortage of water for ore dressing in the summer, and who also got a considerable gain in health from a new month's outdoor labour in the better weather.

Among the many commercial lime-burners in Derbyshire, Farey noted especially the kilns at Calden Law, Ashover, Marple Bridge and Crich, and gives details of their structure. The commercial kiln was greatly increased in height over the field kiln, and there was some experiment in suitable shape. To follow these in detail would lead to a discussion of the modern kiln, which is quite outside the scope of this present account.

To look a little more closely at the smaller running kiln, which we have called the field kiln, it is unlikely that any reader will have an adequate idea of the numbers in which these were built. Notes of limekilns have been kept for some years now, in four particular areas, and the figures might be regarded as impressive and certainly unexpected.

The four areas are the two small valleys of Dentdale and Garsdale, on the west of the Pennines, and Wharfedale and Wensleydale respectively above Hebden and Askrigg.

In these four areas 336 old limekilns have been noted, and these cannot be all that there are, if careful search were made. In Grassington township there are twenty-one, and in Dent township there are at least thirty still to be seen. Nearly all these examples are found just below the outcrop of the thinner limestones of the Yoredale Series, and many of them are not far from the thin coals of the Millstone Grit.

In Wensleydale the limekilns are numerous within fairly easy reach of the Duerley and Snaizeholmedale coal pits, but far less numerous on the same limestones at some distance from easy coal supplies. While the limestone, reasonably good for burning and easy to quarry, was a prime necessity, it was not sufficient in itself. A kiln must have a suitable coal supply, either near at hand or within reasonable reach by small cart or pack ponies.

The coal tracks are a constant feature of our hillsides, leading down from the Millstone Grit edges to the limestone terraces below. Lime was often carried many miles from the kilns, which had a surplus for sale, and Farey noted "the avidity with which Derbyshire farmers search after Limestone of the nature best adapted to their particular soils, and how they toil with it over the hilly roads of an uneven country, to the distance of eight or ten miles; while in many instances the Farmers of Cheshire and Yorkshire come near twice these distances to fetch the Peak lime in Carts; and that by means of the canals it is distributed around from Crich and Peak Forest to the distance of 30, 40, or more miles, for Agricultural purposes, even into the vicinity of and to spread upon calcareous soils . ."

We might reasonably ask the date of many of these kilns and, except in a very general way, that would be a difficult question to answer. The literature already quoted shows that liming was a well-established practice in the seventeenth, and particularly in the eighteenth, centuries.

At Bingley, in Airedale, limestone was burned at an early date, the source being the abundant limestone boulders found in the glacial moraine on which Bingley stands. Speight* after speaking of primitive kilns, says, "Some of these old kilns have been discovered in the course of building operations etc. and many are at present being bared at the excavations in Myrtle Pasture. Two centuries ago lime-burning here was carried on profitably; so much so that there was a continual influx of poor labourers seeking work from other and distant places, and these men, sometimes with their families, settled in the town and became a serious charge on the rates."

From papers in my possession I find that in 1699 the freeholders and other inhabitants of the town petitioned the West Riding Magistrates for relief in this matter, because they said that

> "for a long tyme there have been and now are great quantityes of Lyme Stones gotten promiscuously in Bingley and Micklethwaite, but more especially in Bingley, by means whereof the ground is digged up and very much impaired to

* Speight, H. *Old Bingley*. 1898. p. 241.

the great decay of the yearly value of the same, and also abundance of poor people are drawn to inhabit the said constabulary, soe that the assessment for the poor daily increases to the great burthen and charge of the petitioners."

In 1701 the Justices recognised the rightness of this complaint and issued an order to make a reassessment of the annual value of properties in the constabulary.

Limekilns were also built on the lateral moraine in Wharfedale, the Lanshaw Delves, above Ilkley, and the search for limestone boulders has almost destroyed the original topography of the moraine.

In Giggleswick and Settle townships many limekilns were well established in the eighteenth century, and Brayshaw* notes that farmers in the western part of the parish bought their lime from independent lime-burners who seem to have congregated near Buckhaw Brow. Coal was brought from Fountain Fell, very impure, and gave off a lot of bad gas.

In the eighteenth century there was a small kiln at the foot of Castleberg rock in Settle, and Hutton (*Tour to the Caves*, 1799), says that "limestone was daily got there to supply a kiln at the bottom, the inhabitants had the lime burner presented at the court of the Manor, fearing that if any more was dug out, the rock might fall and bury the whole town in ruins."

Twelve wise and just men were impanelled as jurors and sent to view this impending nuisance, the verdict they returned was that if ever the rock fell it would tumble not towards the town, but the direct contrary way.

Many Turnpike Acts and Enclosure Awards of the later eighteenth century make provision for the carriage of lime, and in the limestone districts it was common to award not more than two acres to a township for getting stone for building, burning into lime, or mending the roads, and occupation roads for leading lime and coal for the improvement of the land, and for that purpose only, are frequently set out in the Award.

The evidence then amounts to this. Limekilns were in general use in the later eighteenth century, but by about the middle of the nineteenth century they were being abandoned. If we say that their main period of usefulness was the century from 1750 to 1850, those will be fairly acceptable round dates, but there will be a period of nearly another century to add before 1750 in which kilns were being built, and their use was gradually spreading over the country.

A few kilns became great commercial ventures, and a very few of the smaller kilns, particularly near the canals, remained in occasional use into the early years of the present century.

The writer remembers as a boy going to the kiln on the canal side to buy a twopenny lump of fresh lime, which usually amounted to near a bucketful, to make whitewash for the annual spring-cleaning.

Lime-burning is now a large-scale technical process, but the older farmers' lime-burning has left the kilns as a pleasant detail in the countryside scene, which blends so much into the hills that its function and long and honourable history is in danger of being lost.

The real monument to the inconspicuous kilns and the men who built and used them is the wide range of sweet upland pasture regained by the free use of lime from sour moorish land.

(November 1960)

* Brayshaw, T. & Robinson, R.M. *History of the Parish of Giggleswick,* 1932, p. 212.

Sutton Stoop   Dan Binns

River Skirfare   Dan Binns

WATER POWER
IN THE DALES

One of the sources of natural power which has been made use of by man from a very early date in his civilisations is that of running and falling water. The water wheel in some form or another has been used from the days of Nineveh and Babylon and was known and used long ago in India, China, Egypt and the near East. In Britain, however, it was only at a comparatively late date that the knowledge of how to make and use water wheels was acquired. There are traces of water wheels on some of the Roman sites in this country, but they are by no means common and the knowledge of them does not seem to have been passed on to the natives.

At the time of the Domesday Survey (1087), water mills had become common in the southern parts of the country and in the Midlands, but were still almost unknown in the country north of the Humber. By the twelfth century water mills were being built in most of the larger manors in the north and were busily at work providing the power for grinding corn.

Our earliest records are thus of mills built by the lord of the manor for his own use and that of his tenants who were generally bound under penalties to grind their corn at the manorial mill and to give service in several ways. In the thirteenth century and later, the growth of the cloth trade led to the building of fulling mills, particularly in the North, and a widespread pattern of mills soon appeared over our streams and rivers.

In later centuries water wheels provided the power for the earliest textile mills, for mine pumping and ore dressing, and for blowing furnaces and working hammers in the iron works.

Most of the wheels have now disappeared but in most cases there remains on the ground traces of either the wheel pit or the leat or race bringing water from stream or dam, and the evidence for those with no visible trace is to be found in a variety of ancient documents.

A search for the location of water wheels in any of our Dales can provide an excuse for happy days of sauntering up and down our numerous streams and can be very rewarding even if the number of wheels discovered is small.

It may come as a surprise to some to learn that on the Wharfe and its tributaries above Bolton Bridge there have been no less than fifty wheels. The search of other dales is still to be completed, but no doubt when it is done we shall have a truer picture of the great part this quiet and unobtrusive source of power has played in dales life. This use of water power is now so shrunken that an active water wheel is worthy of mention in the guide books, and visitors will make a detour to gaze at what is now almost a curiosity.

It would be a large task merely to enumerate the water wheels past and present on the Pennines, and even the modest aim of illustrating the various uses of water for power in one dale can involve a surprising amount of research both indoor and outdoor, and may lead one into many pleasant byways both in the country and in the library.

With its long mining history, the dales area offers a satisfying variety of wheels and any attempt to list them, along with those used in corn and other mills, calls for an outline of many centuries of progress and invention.

The Norman Conquest grafted onto the village custom of Anglo-Danish England a feudal and manorial system in which the lord of the manor had a very privileged position. Among other powers the manorial overlord claimed a monopoly of mills – he alone had the privilege of building and working a corn mill and the tenants on his manor were compelled to grind all their corn at his mill.

This power was not given by any statute or law but was rooted in manorial custom. It was an offence against the manor for a peasant to make or own a hand corn mill or quern, and if such a quern was discovered it was confiscated and often broken and its owner severely fined.

We can learn much about the suit and service of the mill from the grants by which many mills were given to the monasteries as a source of income.

One of the earliest charters relating to a mill concerns the gift by Cecely de Romille, of Silsden corn mill to the canons of Embsay Priory, about 1150, before their removal to the new site at Bolton.

> Let it be known that I have given and conceded and by this present charter confirmed to God and the Blessed Mary, and St. Cuthbert of Embsay and the canons, servants of God there, the mill of Silsden; with all the multure of the said town and all milling services that were due to me, and all liberties and free customs which I have had in connection with the said mill; without any reservation, and in free pure and perpetual alms.
>
> Wherefore no other mill by any other man may be made in the said town save by the will and concession of the said canons. Nor may they (the townsmen) have handmills. If nevertheless any of the said town shall refuse to come to the said mill, I and my heirs shall compel him to follow it: and if any be found attending another mill, the sack and corn shall be the canons', and the horse (carrying the same) as well as the penalty, shall be to me and my heirs . . .

Many contemporary gifts of mills forbade the peasants who owed service to them, to possess a hand mill or quern and in fact any querns discovered were confiscated to the lord of the mill and broken up by the manor steward or disposed of in some other way, sometimes to mend a path or sometimes built into a wall.

This probably explains the frequency of broken querns which in their substance and design seem to be incapable of ever being broken by accident.

The suit and service of the mill included more than just having corn ground there. About 1240 Hugh, son of Hugh of Leathley, gave to the monks of Fountains Abbey "a moiety (or half) of the mill of Rigton to the proper use of the convent, with all its suit and all other appurtenances. The men of Rigton shall maintain the mill dam and the house and bear the carriage of millstones."

The tenants of the manor were to have "free transit to the mill through the territory of Rigton excepting corn and meadow for going and coming to the mill." These "mill paths" are among the oldest paths which are easily recognised and are usually important and well used today because they generally lead to a bridge over the stream or river, a crossing place which in succeeding centuries has become a focus for paths and roads.

The mill needed millstones, and quarries in a suitable rock (often the Millstone Grit, hence the name) were the subject of gifts. About 1211 there is a grant to Fountains Abbey "of all the quarry and all the millstones on Stanybank in the territory of Salley (Sawley near Ripon)... saving to Alan de Aldefield and his heirs reasonable estover of millstones for one mill of Aldefield... but they may not give or sell millstones."

The givers generally reserved a little for themselves from any grant. Castley mill was given with suit and service but with the reservation that the grantor and his heirs shall grind their corn at the same mill without multure – multure being the measure of corn taken by the miller as his due for grinding, and the constant source of grumbling and suspicion against the miller.

The mill dam presented many problems. Although it was not a dam in the modern sense which lifted the level of the water far above its normal level and created a lake of some extent, it was still a barrier to the river, usually a row of stakes with boards between them, often moveable, or it might be a barrier of posts filled in with clay and rubble. These old dams were very often built on a long slant across the river and were intended more for the direction of the water on to the wheel than for holding up a large store of water against drought. In time of flood they were very dangerous in turning the flood on to the mill, and this is remembered in the saying "too much water drowns the miller."

Of course, the dam was liable in a heavy water to flood part of the adjacent banks and it could prove to be a barrier against the free movement of fish upstream. As nearly all riverside manors took as the boundary a line up the middle of the stream course, a dam had of necessity to be built partly on the ground of another manor and so could be the cause of many curious resentments and claims. Early records, both manorial and monastic, are rich in quarrels over the mill dam.

In 1279 the mill at Litton, which had been given to Fountains Abbey some long time previously, became a subject of dispute as the land on the two banks of the river belonged respectively to Fountains and Salley Abbeys. We get the following record of a quarrel:

> ... for the violence and damage done by the monks and lay brothers of Salley to the Abbot of Fountain's mill in Litton they are placed at the amercement (to pay a fine) of the Abbot of Fountains in ten pounds sterling and because the dam of the mill partly extends within the common of the Abbot of Salley, he and his tenants of Litton ought to grind at the mill at the 24th vessel if they wish ...

The offence must have been very serious as a fine of ten pounds sterling would be the equivalent in present cash values of £400 or £500. The Salley Abbey tenants acquired the right, if it were more convenient to them, to grind their corn at Litton mill and thus, in fact saved themselves the trouble of building and maintaining a mill of their own.

Two hundred and fifty years later the monasteries are still involved in mill troubles and here is an example from Richmond in 1537:

> Henry Cogill... about 7 years past purchased and bought a certain land set lying and being in Richemonde in the County of Yorke holden of the king's highness in fee farm, unto the which land belongeth a fresh water upon the which water your orator builded two mills, the building whereof cost your orator the sum of £80 sterling and above And shortly after that your orator had builded the two mills one John, prior of the house of St. Martin in Richmonde, bearing inward malice and displeasure unto your orator and minding utterly to undo him for ever bare your orator over hand that the mid stream of water belonged unto the Abbot of Yorke.

And that the Abbot had commanded him to pull down the dam of the stream, where of right the stream time out of mind belonged and yet doth belong unto the King's highness and his predecessors King of England, yet that notwithstanding for by cause the mills of your orator could not grind if the course of the stream were turned from them, therefor your orator being a poor man and glad to obtain and get the goodwill and favour of the prior compounded with him for the having of the stream and paid unto him for his good will therein £4.13.4d. sterling.

And the prior at the receipt thereof faithfully promised and granted that your orator should peaceably have and enjoy the stream forever. And so it is, right honourable lord, that the prior not regarding his promise right nor good conscience about 4 years past pulled up the dam of the stream, whereby the mills of your orator cannot grind.

And so your orator hath ever since that time lost the profit that might have risen and grown of the mills if the prior had not pulled up the dam of the stream, which is to the utter undoing and impoverishment of your orator for ever unless your lordship's favour to him be showed on this behalf.

And forasmuch as the prior in no wise will permit and suffer your orator to have and enjoy the same according to his promise, nor yet will repay unto your orator the sum of £4.13.4 by him received of your orator as is above said, your orator is compelled of necessity to sue unto your most honourable lordship by bill of petition for reformation of the premises.

On receipt of this petition Robert Bowes and Robert Chaloner were summoned to "take the answer of John prior of St. Martin's to the plea of Henry Cogill, as John is unable to appear in person, to take his attorney and render certificates of their proceeding."

The answer is long and complicated but the essence of it is as follows:

... he saith that one half of the water unto the mid stream as it lieth and hath his course by the ground of the priory appertaineth and belongeth unto the priory as by the grants thereof made more plainly appeareth. And the plaintiff levied and built a dam on the water appertaining to the priory And thereupon relation was made unto William now Abbot, who commanded the defendant to pull down the dam so made levied and builded on the water pertaining to the priory, according to which commandment the prior upon no malice but in the right of the priory and by the commandment of the Abbot in peaceable manner pulled down the mill dam which was fixed and builded on the water belonging to the monastery as lawful was for him to do ...

The prior also says no promises were ever made or payments accepted, and concludes with a masterpiece of jargon

And without that that any other thing material specified in the bill and in this answer not confessed or denied is true.

The prior made a plea for discharge with costs but unfortunately the result of the plea is not known. Among other things it would be good to know what is meant when it is said that the prior pulled down the dam *in peaceable manner*.

This was by no means the first mill dispute near Richmond. In 1162 Torfin gave to Easby Abbey seven acres on which to make a sheepfold and a quit claim of the mill, its site and pool, near the wood of Easby, about which there had been a dispute between them.

The monastic houses although forbidden in the Cistercian General Chapter as early as 1191 to accept the appropriation of mills, still continued to covet and accept the gift of mills, not only as an unfailing source of revenue but as a means of keeping a permanent contact with the whole population of a manor, all of whom could be compelled to come to the mill.

The mill rights were jealously guarded, as we see, for example, at Bolton Priory in 1233.

> Agreement between Richard the Prior and Giles Mauleverer who gave the dam of their mill pool below their garden in land in Twyselwatholm, and lest another mill should be erected there the priory granted him the right to grind his corn without multure and to his men the same rights as his brother's men had in Storith.

Cecily Romille about 1150 gave to Embsay Priory the vill of Kildwick with the mill and its *soke* and in nearly all the gifts of mills the gift specifies the mill with suit and service, or soke. Soke is derived from the Saxon word *soc*, a privilege or liberty, and *soca*, the area or district over which such a privilege extended. The tenant of a soke mill was a *socman*.

The word soke came to mean both the privilege and the area to which it applied. The soke of a mill included the right to prevent any other mill being built in the same manor and the power to compel the tenants of the manor to grind all their corn at the soke mill. This in effect created a valuable monopoly without any period specified for its duration.

It is perhaps surprising that the privilege of soke does not rest in law but only in custom, and it is nearly impossible to get rid of a soke obligation except by an outright purchase and a voluntary extinction by the purchaser. If one looks ahead it can be seen that by the enforcement of the soke monopoly, it might become a valuable source of income forever.

When Wakefield finally got rid of the soke of the manor mills, as late as 1854, the cost was more than £21,500 authorised by a special Act of Parliament as a rate on the whole of the property owners living within the soke; 1s. 6d. in the pound was levied on breweries, hotels and taverns, 8d. in the pound on combined shops and houses, 10d. on dwelling-houses of £5 rateable value or more, 5d. on maltkilns and flour mills, 3d. on general manufacturers, public buildings, offices, etc., and so on down to a penny in the pound on railways, canals and land liable to poor rates.

The rate was enforceable by law and by distraint for recovery.

The Bradford soke mill was bought by the corporation and the railways in 1871 for £19,000 and all the soke rights were extinguished. The soke of Leeds mill cost £13,000 in 1839. These large sums were paid, as the Wakefield Act says, so that all the tenants and inhabitants were freed from the obligation of grinding at the mill and so that any other mills could be built in the soke area such as "steam-mills, windmills, watermills, horsemills, handmills, querns, . . . etc."

The great price paid was for the soke rights only. The mill property and estate were not included in the sale. This, perhaps as much as anything, illustrates the powerful position held by the holder of the soke, throughout the middle and later ages.

Now let us have a look at the mill and the river and see how much we can learn about them. A mill among its other rights has in the course of time acquired a claim on the water and nothing may be done to a stream which would diminish the flow of water to a mill.

As this applies to all the mills on a stream or river it follows that each mill only has the *use* of the water as it passes. Whatever is led from the stream to the mill must return to the stream. In most cases therefore a mill built beside a stream or river has a head race or goit leading water to the mill, and a tail race or goit carrying it back to the river below the mill.

These goits often remain when all else has disappeared and can be recognised even if silted in and overgrown. They are often the first clue to be looked for along a stream bank.

The mill and the wheel were most likely to have been replaced a century or more ago by large structures and no trace of them will be found, only the modern successor marking the position of an old mill. The mills were small and many of the wheels were undershot with the stream running under and not over them.

The wheels were of small diameter not more than five or six feet generally, and much broader than more modern ones. They were built over the stream of water which impinged on the wheel paddles which were little more than straight boards.

A drawing of 1340 shows a mill with an overshot wheel in which the water is delivered at the top of the wheel and its weight in the buckets or segments of the wheel gives the driving power. This type of wheel is usually associated with a dam to maintain a steady flow of water, and is more characteristic of slow flowing lowland streams. In the undershot wheel the speed of the water matters most and so a swift upland stream is very suitable for them.

The wheel turned a top millstone of a pair and did not need very great power. The building for such a mill would be quite small, built in timber, and not likely to leave much trace when it decayed or was replaced.

The monastic and manorial corn mills will thus depend for their discovery on work in the library, but when a list is prepared the ground should be examined and attention might usefully be given to field names such as Mill Gill, Mill Field, Mill Scar Lash and so on. All clues and records should be transferred to a map such as the one given in this article.

Mills utilised any good supply of water and at Linton there is an interesting example of three mills close together, each using a different kind of supply. Linton Mill has a long slant dam on the river and uses a portion of deflected river water; Threshfield mill (Billy Gudgeon mill) is near the river but takes water by a long goit from Captain Beck into a small dam against the mill; Grassington Low mill, opposite the church, uses the water from Brow Well, a spring of very large volume and fairly constant flow.

The details of these supplies can still be seen in each case, with a little trouble.

The greatest period of the water corn mills was roughly from the thirteenth to the late eighteenth century, when steam-driven flour mills near the ports began to displace the small country mills. Many milling firms were established in the market towns near the corn-growing areas, and when grain began to be imported into the country in quantity, even these began to decline in favour of the mills in Liverpool, London and other ports.

This migration of corn-milling from some of the rural areas and the decline of corn-growing on most of the upland country and particularly on the Pennines, left a number of small water mills with their valuable water rights available for other uses. It was this available power that formed an important factor in the early textile revolution.

The first process in woollen manufacture to be adapted to a power drive, was that of fulling the newly-woven cloth. In the earlier days, after weaving the web, the cloth was cleaned of grease and oil and when made of short staple wool (short fibres) it was kneaded in water to felt and thicken it and also to shrink it. At first the cloth was trampled in water, either in a stream or in troughs, the fuller stamping it with his feet and so getting the name of a "walker," and the place for this kind of work was a "walk mill." The relative abundance of the surname Walker, derived from this occupation, is evidence of its age and importance. The surname Fuller also commemorates the process.

The earlier fulling mills were established near communities of cloth makers as one fuller could serve many weavers. Fulling mills were thus set up near Leeds, Halifax, Wakefield and the other growing woollen towns, as well as smaller mills near or in villages with a number of weavers.

At Kilnsey grange of Fountains Abbey, in Wharfedale, the centre of its extensive Craven sheep farms, there was a fulling mill alongside its corn mill, at the place on the river still called Mill Scar Lash. These mills were at work in the fourteenth century. In the Poll Tax survey of 1379 persons described as "fuller" are taxed in Keighley, Skipton (2), Hanlith, Coniston Cold, Preston, Gargrave (2), Flasby, Kirkby Malham, Addingham, Hebden, Linton and Appletreewick, and in Threshfield, Hartlington, Draughton, Steeton and several other villages, one person has the surname Walker. In Gargrave, Skipton and Keighley there are Thomas, William and John Walker, all of them described as fullers.

The fuller used a natural detergent to degrease the cloth, the so called "fuller's earth," which occurs as a regular geological deposit in many parts of the country and which was quarried and sent to the markets for the supply of the fullers. This remained the common detergent until very recent times. About the end of the twelfth century a mechanised method of fulling was introduced, using wooden mallets or stamps lifted by cogs on a shaft turned by a water wheel and allowed to fall on the cloth in a trough of water. The earliest such mills of which there is still a record include one at Newsham, in Yorkshire, in the year 1185.

The new fulling mills were sometimes placed alongside an existing corn mill, as at Kilnsey, and could use the same water and have advantage of the mill paths, but most of the mills were placed at new sites. The three essentials for the fulling mill were water for power, a group of village weavers to serve, and a good track by which the finished cloth could be carried to market. Although the cloths were carried by the weavers to the mill in single pieces, the fuller usually accumulated a number of cloths after fulling, and the next stage of their journey was to the nearest cloth market.

The development of fulling mills continued as the cloth trade increased, but most of the new mills were established near the growing towns and the cloth centres. The clothiers in general put out yarn to be woven in the cottages over a wide area and collected the woven cloth in the "grey" unscoured condition, then either finished it themselves or put it out to the fuller to be finished in quantity. Their shops grew up near the river, particularly in the new cloth areas around the Calder and Colne valleys. In the Dales the water mills were little affected until the end of the eighteenth century and in the opening of the nineteenth century when other textile processes were mechanised.

The first great change in cloth-making came with the invention in 1733 of Kaye's "flying shuttle." The weaver sent the shuttle from hand to hand through the shedded warp, but Kaye made two "picks" which could throw the shuttle across the loom with the motion of strings operated with one hand, leaving the other to work the beam. This quickened up the whole process so much that the home spinners were no longer able to keep pace with the needs of the weavers, and pressure was put on the demand for a speedier way of spinning.

The next important inventions were a natural outcome of this demand. In succession there came Hargreave's spinning frame in 1764, by which at first eight threads, and later, as many as eighty, could be spun at once. This frame was turned by hand. In 1769 Arkwright made his spinning "jenny," and in 1774 the Crompton "mule" spinning frame was completed in workable form. In all these machines, multiple threads were spun at the same time, and the limit to the number seemed to be the effort taken to turn the machine. Arkwright saw the possibility of using water power, and his "water frame" was operated by a small water wheel.

Arkwright's and Crompton's frames were soon improved, and it became imperative to use water power for their driving force. The steam engine had been in use for a long time for pumping, but it was not yet used directly for a rotative motion, and in any case was large and expensive and used very large amounts of coal.

Smeaton, the Yorkshire-born engineer, builder of the Eddystone Lighthouse, had improved the water wheel to develop more power, but even he, with steam power to hand, used the steam engine to pump water on to the water wheel, which was to be used for winding at the Benton Colliery. The improved design, mainly in the overshot wheel in which the water runs on to the wheel near its highest point, provided a new and cheap source of power wherever there was a good stream of water.

The spinners already had large businesses as "putters out" – taking wool to cottage spinners and collecting spun yarn from them, thus spending time and effort in much travelling over scattered areas of farms and cottages. They saw the double advantage of the new frames in greatly increased business and concentration of the work on one spot.

These inventions coincide with another social revolution which had just begun and was rapidly gaining momentum, the enclosure movement. The old systems of agriculture were being altered and common lands and common fields were being enclosed, sheep and cattle rearing were extending in the hill country and corn was being brought in from the lowland areas, with the resultant reduction in the number of labourers needed on the land.

The displaced agricultural families provided a source of labour for the new type of spinner, who brought his frames together into a factory where water power was available. The new type of building took over the old name and became a "mill" though no milling was done there. It was natural to look to some of the existing water corn mills, many of which were experiencing a steady decline in trade, but which had ancient and valuable water rights. Many of the older mills changed over from corn to textiles, and many newer mills were built, often crowded fairly close together on a good stream which was not liable to too severe summer droughts.

These inventions in spinning were made in the cotton area of Lancashire at a time when water power was about the only economic source of power. The turnpike roads and the Leeds and Liverpool Canal (though not completed right across the Pennines until 1816, it was linked with a short overland carriage by wagon from Burnley to Gargrave) brought Lancashire and Yorkshire into close contact so that the cotton trade was able to extend its sphere of influence at least as far east as Skipton.

Skipton was linked by the canal with Leeds and Bradford, but a lot of its traffic was lime and limestone, manures, etc., from Craven, with return loads of coal, iron and merchandise, and did not really bring Skipton into the woollen area. The result of the Lancashire connection was that people like the Dewhurst brothers, and others before them, set up cotton spinning mills on the watercourses in the Dales near Skipton. Thus there were five mills on Embsay Beck: Whitfield Sike Mill, Good Intent Mill, Sandbank Mill, Primrose Mill, and Mill Holme, all of them by 1850 spinning cotton and three of them cotton-spinners in 1820, one a worsted spinning mill, and one a corn mill.

These mills were influenced in their location by the nearness to Skipton and the canal and roads, and by the excellent flow of the stream. All were water wheel driven. There were cotton-spinning water mills also at Arncliffe, Cononley, Coniston Cold, Earby, Eastby, Kettlewell, Kirkby Malham and Langcliffe. The Birkbecks of Settle had a worsted mill at Linton, and there were worsted mills at Addingham, Burley, Kildwick and Cross Hills, locations nearer to the woollen and worsted areas on the east.

Most of these cotton-spinning mills were still in operation at the mid-nineteenth century, but as steam power became available near the canal, which could bring coal from the coalfields of either Yorkshire or Lancashire, they gradually gave way to the new and larger mills along the line of the canal. The water power was not capable of much increase, so that a business based on one of the Dales mills had little prospect of growing.

The Dewhurst brothers are typical, transferring their energies to new and large mills at Skipton, built against the canal, and giving up their commitments at Embsay and Kirkby Malham.

There was a traditional textile industry to the east of the Pennines, which had considerable influence on the story of the Dales water mills, the spinning of flax and weaving of linen. In the eighteenth century, Knaresborough was one of the very important centres of this industry, and in fact, in 1824, an account of the town notes this trade as employing 800 flax dressers and 1,300 linen weavers in Knaresborough. Like the cotton trade, the linen trade found it a great improvement when flax spinning could be concentrated in mills using the spinning frames, rather than having to carry out the dressed flax to hundreds of scattered homes to be spun on the old wheel. The obvious area for this development was the valley of Nidd, so that we find a large number of water mills being converted or built for the flax spinning.

Pateley Bridge became a subsidiary linen centre for a while, and flax dressing and spinning, with the spinning of hemp coming later, became an industry in its own right in Nidderdale. In Pateley Bridge in 1822 there were five linen manufacturers and four flax spinners, with ten linen manufacturers and two flax spinners at Dacre, four linen manufacturers and a flax spinner at Darley, flax spinners at Blubberhouses, two linen manufacturers at Hampsthwaite and at Hartwith, and two flax spinners at Hartwith also.

These are not all, but indicate something of the way this trade invaded the Nidd Valley, using its water power. A small colony of flax spinners soon occupied the upper streams of the Washburn where at West End, on Capelshaw Beck, there were High Mill, Little Mill and Patrick's Mill, and Low Mill and Blubberhouse West House Mill on the Washburn, all spinning flax.

It is not the purpose of this article to trace the history either of the cotton or the linen trade, however tempting and interesting it might be, but to display these trades as responsible for a large number of water wheels being built in the Dales, many of which can still be traced. Between them, corn grinding, flax spinning and cotton spinning have been responsible for a few score of wheels, and a complete list of them would be of great interest and would indicate a period when the water power of the Dales was a factor of very great economic importance.

In the Pennines, around the Calder and further south, there was a development of paper-making, mainly for the packing demands of the textile industries, and based upon not only the water power, but on the great demand that trade makes upon supplies of pure and soft water. Paper-making extended a little into the Dales and has left two permanent marks, the paper mills at Langcliffe, near Settle, and the paper mill at Skyreholme, near Appletreewick. At this latter mill there is still to be seen one of the finest of the Dales' water wheels.

A great many of the water mills which for a time were employed in cotton or flax or even in corn, have ceased to operate in these materials in the latter part of the last century, and have turned to another local resource, timber, and become saw mills, estate mills, or joinery works, still using the old water wheels for power. It is to be hoped that some will continue to work so that young folk of today may have a chance to see in operation what was, a century and more ago, a prime source of power on which much of the early industry was based.

(January and March 1961)

BUILDINGS
OF THE DALES

Bainbridge

John F. Greenwood

DALES BUILDING OF THE SIXTEENTH AND SEVENTEENTH CENTURIES

1. Bridges

The Pennine areas of Yorkshire and the borders of Derbyshire and East Lancashire are unusually rich, among other things, in picturesque villages and fine river scenery; both of them frequently enhanced by the art and skill of builders of a former period, from whom we inherit the very dignified and attractive seventeenth century stone-roofed, mullioned-windowed cottages, the fine yeoman houses – "Halls" and "Manor Houses" now – and some famous river bridges. Descriptive references to these features are numerous, but surprisingly little has been written or said about their builders and designers, or the social and economic factors which produced them. I propose to deal briefly with the builders and the building of the dales bridges, halls, and cottages, embarrassed rather than helped by the wealth of illustrative detail from which selection must be made.

The earliest period of extensive stone building, in common with the rest of the country, is that of the 12th and 13th centuries, to which period the early parts of most of our castles and abbeys belong. In this building and in the repair and extension of the work produced, large companies of skilled masons and stone workers were in constant employment until the early 16th century, when the shadow of the impending dissolution of the monasteries and the relative peace following the settlement of the Welsh and Scottish Border troubles slowed down the building work on monastic and military sites respectively. By the middle of the century both were virtually at an end.

During the half century following the dissolution (this was completed in the period 1535-1540) building was mainly confined to bridges and to larger halls, but with the opening of the seventeenth century came a period of building "boom" when stone houses replaced timber and wattle structures, both in the larger "hall" and in humbler cottages. There is a definite link and development through these different phases, that can be traced if we consider the bridges and cottages of the dales area and their builders.

First we must glance at the builders of the later monastic period. It is clear from a study of the Fabric Rolls – building and clerk-of-works department accounts – of York Minster and others of the monastic churches, that there was a definite organisation to deal with repairs and extensions to the mother church, and also on all the estates appertaining to it. A master mason was elected by the monastic authorities, usually the Chapter, who was very much in the position of a bailiff, receiving their orders, submitting estimates, and making contracts, employing men, buying materials and rendering accounts for their inspection. He employed a number of masons – master masons, rough masons, and apprentices – quarrymen and labourers, and occasionally plasterers. A similar position was frequently held by a master carpenter, who employed woodmen, sawyers, carpenters and labourers.

The masons' department usually either owned or leased quarries for their stone getting – York Minster Chapter had quarries at Thevedale, Huddleston, Stapleton and Bramham, where they employed one or two quarrymen permanently, and sent extra men to work for a few weeks at busy periods. The stone was got, and rough dressed with picks or stone-axe, at the quarry before being sent to the mason's lodge at York for final dressing and use. Kirkstall Abbey had both leases and gifts of quarries in Bramley Fall and their masons were assisted by a few permanent stone hewers. The masons and apprentices lived in a "lodge" which usually included several rooms or buildings on the site of their work, and were bound by many rules and regulations in their conduct and workmanship. After a seven years' apprenticeship, a man could, after examination and testing of his craft and skill, become a free mason capable of being employed directly as an independent workman on any job. Rough masons were essentially workers in plain stone building and walling, the free masons usually adding to this skill in carving and working in "free-stone". On election as a free mason, a mark was adopted by each individual, by which his work was often identified and which sometimes was used in the signing of contracts.

Following the dissolution of the monasteries large numbers of masons who had been servants of the religious houses were turned out of their occupation, and formed themselves into bands or "lodges" which wandered about the country taking contracts to build bridges, houses, or restore churches, etc., and spreading abroad the traditions of monastic building and design. The groups kept to their "lodges" and maintained their rules and orders, under a master mason who became lodge-master and foreman.

A few such bands of masons were available for secular work during the monastic period, and some records of their methods remain to us. A contract was made in 1421, between seven local gentry and three masons, Thomas Ampleforthe, John Garrett and Robert Maunsell, "to make a brigg of stane oure ye water of Swalle atte Catrik (Catterick) betwixt ye olde stane brigg and ye Newbrigge of tre (timber)... sufficient and workmanly in Masoncraft accordand in substance to Barnacastell brigge..."

The bridge was to have two piers, three arches, land abutments, parapets, etc., and the masons to get their stone from two quarries about four miles away, one on each side of the river; they were to find all limestone and sand, to build limekilns and get what wood and "colles" were needed to "birn" their lime; they were to get all timber needed for piles, dams, centring for the arches, and all other purposes and to provide carriage for all stone, lime, fuel, sand, and timber "so gotten." The trustees who made the contract bound themselves to provide a wooden lodge with various rooms in which the masons could live and work, a store room for the tools, and necessary storage space. The bridge was to be completed in four years for a payment of 260 marks (about £175) and each year a gown given to each mason according to his degree. A similar contract had been made in 1412 for the rebuilding of Catterick Church.

An earlier contract between Sir Richard Scrope and John Lewyn, master mason, for building Bolton Castle, Wensleydale, was made in 1378, but the two contracting parties shared more of the work. Lord Scrope provided all the timber for the structure and for lime burning, and all carriage of materials; Lewyn was to get all stone, lime and sand, and was paid 100 shillings per perch of walling, with a payment on completion of 50 marks. Long timbers were required for the roof and floors and it is recorded that "most parte of the Tymber was fett out of the Forest of Engleby in Cumberland, and Richard Lord Scrope for conveyance of itt, had layde by the wey dyvers draughts of oxen to carry it from place to place till it come to Bolton." It was frequently the case that sites on the Pennines were unable to provide long timbers, and these were brought from considerable distance, sometimes from the Vale of Eden, sometimes as far as Sherwood Forest.

These two contracts are illustrative of a general procedure at that period – a person or group proposing to build either hall, chapel, or bridge, employed a master mason to take charge of the work and assume all responsibilities, and in addition to get some or all of the materials. The master mason contractor sometimes provided a model of his proposed work and almost certainly in most cases provided the design, thus bringing about the close similarity and persistence of design over a wide area and a long period, that has become crystallised as a "local traditional" style. He employed masons for the stone cutting and building, labourers and apprentices who quarried stone, burnt lime, made mortar and did other jobs on the material, timber men and carpenters for the timber work, and a blacksmith for the care of the tools and to make iron-work – cramps, nails, door furnishings, and so on. In some cases contracts for the making of the roof with its timber work and stone slating or lead flashing were let by separate tender to a group of craftsmen. Whether the roof was leaded or stone slated, the term used in all the contracts is "thekyng" and we get such terms as "thekyd with stane sclates" and "thekyng with lede."

As the monasteries had widely scattered estates, with their farms, mills, granges and moors, they frequently built or maintained bridges along their roads, and usually had one or more master masons in charge of a repair gang which could be sent out to build or repair on their properties. Salley Abbey had a bridge at Salley (now Sawley) and an early benefactor gave it an annual rent charge for two shillings on some land, to provide for its repair. In 1305 Bolton Priory spent £21:12:9 in building "the bridge at Kyldwyk," over the Aire and the work can still be seen in the western side of the present structure. Older bridges than this are by no means common, but there are at least a few that are contemporary. The little bridge at Bow Bridge near Askrigg is 13th century, the "Devil's Bridge" at Kirkby Lonsdale was repaired in 1275 and the bridge at Marske in Swaledale may be early monastic. Many others will be called to the mind of the reader. These early bridges are all built on a ribbed understructure, a pattern that remained in use for about three centuries.

Until the 16th century the provision and maintenance of bridges was largely dependant upon local needs and the exertions of the manorial overlords, secular or monastic, but in 1530 the situation had become one of national urgency and a statute (Hen. VIII, 22, ch. 5) was enacted empowering the local Justices of the Peace to enquire "of all manner of annoyances of bridges broken in the highways to the damage of the Kings liege people" and to estimate the cost of repair or replacement and levy the same on the appropriate district; they were also instructed to appoint surveyors to examine and oversee the work. Proceedings under this Act were taken at the Quarter Sessions, but were very slow to begin in the north, and it was not until long after the end of the monasteries that a period of extensive bridge building was initiated.

The sixteenth century was a period of expanding trade and prosperity when agriculture flourished and markets became of the greatest importance. On the suppression of the religious orders the great monastic estates were valued and sold, many of them to merchant speculators, and some to the wealthier titled families, often relatives of the last abbot.

The purchaser generally cut out of the estates a park and site for a mansion, with demesne and farms, forest or waste for hunting, and all the essentials of a country seat. The displaced masons were employed to build a hall, using the monastic buildings as a quarry for cut stone, and sometimes (as at Bolton Priory) incorporating part of the secular buildings in the hall. The outlying estates with their numerous farms and granges were mostly broken up and sold off sooner or later to the tenants who had worked on them under the monks.

Thus a minor social revolution was achieved – the translation of thousands of tenant farmers into small freeholders. Two generations of the new freehold ownership during a period of national and agricultural prosperity sufficed to ensure a modicum of wealth and a sense of dignity and pride of family to most of the freeholders, and these found natural expression in the replacement of small timber dwellings by substantial stone dwellings, worthy of the newly established family dignity. The monastic farms had sent most of their produce into the barns and store houses of the abbey granges and one of the first necessities on the new freeholds was the provision of farm buildings. In this urgent building the humbler of the masons and carpenters would find employment, while their more skilled comrades were at work on the halls and mansions.

It is often noticeable that a seventeenth century farm has a late sixteenth century barn or out-buildings, often with fine timber roof, and this is to be expected; the farmer could always manage a little longer in his house, however small and inconvenient, but it was essential that his stock should be well housed and his hay crops protected if he were to prosper in his new venture.

Towards the end of the sixteenth century work on the abbey sites and larger halls was slowing down, and the masons so released, with their new generations of apprentices, were quickly absorbed in meeting the demand for farm buildings, bridges, and the earliest of the new houses. As trade and markets increased, roads and bridges became essential, and Quarter Sessions took an increasing interest in the reports of their surveyors. Many old bridges were of timber and in ruinous or unsafe condition. In 1602 the bridges over the Wharfe at Linton (Grassington) and Burnsall were reported as ruinous and in great need of repairs; horses and carriages could only cross with great labour and danger. Justices were to enquire which parts of the West Riding could bear the cost of rebuilding, but in the end Linton Bridge was rebuilt by public levy, and Burnsall Bridge was rebuilt later, 1609, at the sole cost of Sir William Craven. In 1612 Ingleton bridge was repaired with the proceeds of a levy of £60 on the West Riding; Silsden and Thornton bridges were similarly repaired in 1613 and in 1615 Coniston (Wharfedale) bridge was granted £30 to be levied on the West Riding "but never to be charged more."

Year by year the surveyors reported and repaired the older bridges, and these reports contain some startling reminders of the changes that have taken place in our main lines of traffic. The Gargrave bridge reports have many features of interest. After reporting it ruinous and needing more than £300 to repair it, the surveyor goes on to say "to rebuilt that bridge of stone, which must of necessity be soe, because there is noe tymber in that parte of the country fitt for that worke, and the said bridge beinge soe usefull and comodious for the whole countrye, beinge the high road betweene the citye of London and the countryes of Westmorland and Cumberland..." As it was not known who ought to repair it, £200 was levied on the wapentakes of Staincliffe, Ewcross and Claro, and the residue on the West Riding. The new stone bridge was completed, after three years work, in 1641 and as all the money raised had not been used, small grants were made for the completion of work at Elslack and other smaller bridges.

The bridge at Hubberholme, Wharfedale, is noted as "beinge the high roade way leadinge between the markett towne of Lancaster in the countie of Lancaster, and the markett towne of Newcastle-upon-Tyne and other places in the countie of Northumberland..." The road indicated would be a fairly direct line by Clapham – Helwith Bridge (repaired 1611) – Greenfield – Hubberholme, then by Wensleydale, Richmond and Durham. The bridge was repaired at the cost of the wapentakes in 1639. Barden Bridge is reported on in 1659 as "not beinge knowne who ought to repaire itt, ordered a greate summe upon ye W.R. beinge £300." It was destroyed soon after, in the floods of 1673 and again rebuilt at the cost of the West Riding in 1676.

It is perhaps sufficient to say in summary that the first fifty years of the seventeenth century saw nearly all the main bridges of the West Riding either repaired or rebuilt in stone, on the site of earlier bridges, generally of wood. Time after time the lack of timber suitable for the repairs is noted, and orders made for a "new brigg of stone." The seventeenth century work and some that is earlier is to be seen in most of the bridges if looked at underneath; the old narrow arch is incorporated in the present wider bridge, and is sometimes built on ribs. The arch is often of different curvature from the newer part.

On the older portions it is common to find mason marks, principally on the finer tooled stones of the arches. On a single bridge there is often considerable variety, ten or a dozen different marks being found, though in many cases there are fewer. As mentioned earlier, these marks indicate the work of different masons, who did the dressing and shaping, and enabled the master mason to keep a check on the work of his men and to assess it either for praise and payment or for blame. From the number of different marks on the larger bridges it seems that the "lodge" may have numbered from 12 to 15 master masons, with their attendant apprentices and labourers, possibly 25 to 30 in all. In a few cases, similar marks appear on different bridges, which may mean that the same men worked on both jobs, or an apprentice may have adopted his master's mark; on the other hand the marks are fairly simple, as they are cut with a fine, shallow line in the face of the stone, and some of them are widely used, and duplicated over many centuries. The earliest mason marks appear on some work of the twelfth century, both in this country and abroad, but they become most frequent in the fifteenth and sixteenth centuries. A few examples are added, from these periods, and from some local bridges, but the whole collection from our Yorkshire buildings would occupy a small volume for publication.

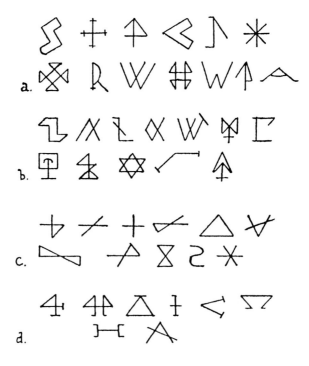

Examples of Mason Marks

(a)   Catterick Bridge, 1421
(b)   Bolton Priory W. tower, 1520
(c)   Linton Bridge, 1602.
(d)   Barden Bridge, 1676.

2. Cottages

The rapid extension of bridge building and repairs in the late sixteenth and early seventeenth centuries concurrent with expanding markets and a period of general prosperity effected great changes in the economic condition and life of the small farmers in the Dales. As was shown by many of the early bridge reports, highways between the larger markets traversed practically the whole of the Dales area, and along them teams of pack-horses provided a ready means of transport for any surplus goods from local farms – cheese, wool, and hides – and an easy route by which stock could be driven to sale.

   These facilities were symptomatic of an important social and economic change that was sweeping slowly over the whole countryside. The manorial system of farming that had been followed for 800 years was breaking down, and its rigid traditional methods were strongly challenged by experiment along many lines. The enclosure of common-fields had begun in many parishes, by private agreement, and was carried out to a considerable extent during the reign of Elizabeth, particularly in the southern and midland counties, while the north was more affected by the expansion of the trade in wool and in the increased utilisation of its uplands for sheep pasture. While rising prices which followed the new trade served to increase the poverty of the labouring classes, they considerably helped the new freeholders who were living largely on the produce of their own land, and selling wool and other goods in the open markets – they were enabled to accumulate cash wealth with which they could pay for the labour of masons, builders, carpenters, and other craftsmen, for work necessary for the better housing of themselves and their stock.

The housing of the agricultural population prior to the seventeenth century was very crude and inadequate; small hovels built on "crucks" – a framework of oak beams – with wattle or turf walls, thatched roof and earthen floor, with an open fire and a hole in the roof for the escape of some of the smoke, were general. Bishop Hall says of the small farmer's house, that it is

> "One of bay's breadth, God whot a silly cote,
> Whose thatched spars are furred with sluttish soote
> A whole inch thick, shining like blackmoor's brows
> Through smoke that down the headlesse barrel blows.
> At his bed's feete feeden his stalled teame,
> His swine beneath, his pullen o'er the beame"

The "bay's breadth" is about 16 to 18 feet, the space needed for stalling an ox team – the "headless barrel" formed the chimney, placed in the thatch and lined with clay. Occasionally the chimney was made of wattle daubed with clay, a good example being altered only recently in the township of Threshfield. A description in 1621 (William Webster) of the Cheshire yeoman farmers says "they had their fire in the midst of the house against a hob of clay, and their oxen also under the same roof; but within these forty years it is altogether altered, so that they have built chimneys, and furnished other parts of their houses accordingly." This change to better houses began with the latter part of the sixteenth century, as Harrison mentions in his Description of England, 1577, when speaking of the new race of prosperous farmers – "every man turned builder, pulled downe the old house and set up a new after his owne divise."

In the northern districts there was an insufficient supply of long timbers for the new and larger houses, but there was no lack of good stone for walls and roof slates, and with a large number of skilled masons and builders recently employed on bridges and monastic buildings now wandering the country seeking employment, it was inevitable that there should be initiated in our Dales a period of extensive stone building. A fairly widespread custom of inscribing dates and initials on the new houses provides invaluable material for the student of the rehousing, and has made it possible to compare a long series of accurately dated buildings. The date stones range from about 1570 to 1720, with most in the period 1640 – 1670. Comparison of a few hundred of these dated houses reveals many common elements of plan and structure, with remarkable individuality preserved and emphasised in the details of design and ornament.

The "crucked" houses were usually one bay's length, that is about 16 feet by 10 feet and the single room served all purposes, except that occasionally a few boards laid across the ties would provide a small loft for stores or for extra sleeping room. In the stone building period it has already been mentioned that the farmer provided first for his stock and his hay by building barns and cowsheds, thus leaving the house free to be used for family purposes only. The new plan was usually a house of two or three bays, the largest room being the living room or "house place." This was often rather larger than the traditional bay, 18 feet by 12 feet being a common size. It was furnished with the principal fireplace, a large "ingle" with wide chimney and large, roomy chimney breast, which accommodated an open wood or peat fire.

Often at one side, built against the chimney or even projecting through if the wall was an outside one, and seen outside as a semicircular "buttress," was the stone oven for baking bread, heated by burning brushwood inside it till it was hot enough, then brushing out the ashes and using the heat stored in the massive stonework for completing the baking, with a "cooling oven." The chimney ingle was generally provided with a wrought iron chimney crane and pot hooks to hold pots and cauldrons over the open fire, and these were often pieces of excellent design and good smith craft. The main door of the house usually opened opposite one side of the chimney breast making the small space shut off between the side of the ingle and the outer wall, in effect, a porch. Out of the living room opened, at the side opposite the fireplace, a back kitchen or dairy, with pantry cut off on the north side. Behind the fireplace there was sometimes a third room, the parlour, also with fireplace, smaller and more ornate than that of the living room. All the floors were made with stone flags, kept clean with crushed sand; some readers may remember in their youth the painful hours spent "crushing sand" from well decayed sandstone, often carted and sold at a small price for this purpose by itinerant dealers who also sold "scouring stone, white and yellow," for the decoration of the fireplace and steps.

The building ranged as near east and west as was practicable, with mullioned windows to all rooms on the south side. The house was rarely placed on a prominent "view point", but with wisdom born of bitter experience of our climate nestled below a shoulder of hill, glad of shelter on the north and east side and very conservative of any gleam of direct sunlight that could be entrapped into the house for light and warmth.

A second storey was made by carrying up the party walls to the roof, and flooring the upstairs with broad oak planks pegged on to oak joists and beams. These floors were not underdrawn but beams and joists were open to the rooms beneath, and often formed an important factor in the general attractiveness of the seventeenth century room. The bedrooms opened one out of the other, the stairs being generally of stone and along the north wall at the rear of the dairy or parlour. The rooms were not ceiled, being open to the roof timbers. Water supply for the house was by a well or pump in the dairy, or a sink to which rain water from large collecting tanks was piped. In the case of a cluster of houses in a hamlet or village there may have been a common supply at a well or spring, to be fetched and carried.

Over the whole of the Pennines there is very little variation from this plan and arrangement in the smaller houses and cottages of this period, strong evidence that it was practical and suited to the life and customs of the times, and already "traditional."

Accounts of the actual building of some of these houses are rare and meagre, but sufficient can be gleaned from them and from the structure and materials used, to understand the general procedure. In many cases the site was already determined by a pre-existing "crucked" house, and the same site or any close at hand was utilised. Fortunately in many cases the older house was retained as an outhouse, and many examples have only disappeared in recent years. A master mason, with one or two masons or apprentices, would be called in to contract for the building and for the bulk of the materials to be found. The foundations were prepared simply by stripping the turf, and by rolling into place large footing stones, bedded on gravel. In many houses examined while under repair, or alteration, it has been noted that the foundations are not much more than a foot below the inside floor level, and the foundation-course stones may be as large as 3 or 4 feet by 2 feet by 2 feet, large partly-rounded boulders rolled off the fields, if necessary roughly squared with the large hammer or maul. This basal course is often 4 feet thick.

1641

1678

1675

JR.

The walls were built, in the limestone areas, of partially rounded rough limestone and sandstone boulders taken from the fields or river bed, built as a double wall, rubble filled and bound together with abundant "throughs," with the corners and opening frames made with squared sandstone. The provision of suitable stone for throughs and corners, window and door jambs, cills and lintels, sustained a small quarrying industry, as the same stone is used over fairly wide districts, and can often be traced to its particular quarry. The lower beds of the Millstone Grit that caps many of the Dales fells has been the stone most commonly used, and from many overgrown quarries on the fell edges, lines of deep-cut packhorse tracks give evidence of the extensive trade formerly carried on there. It seems probable from the few accounts we have, that the stone was brought rough, and cut on the building site by the master mason*. There is surprisingly little fine debris to be found near the quarries. The roughing out at the quarry is referred to as "scappeling" and stones are often bought as "scappeled," that is rough dressed with pick and hammer. The mortar used in building was made from lime locally burned, and as most villages had a lime pit and kiln adjacent, used for liming the land, mortar was easily obtained. Much of the old mortar examined is made of lime and sand, ashes being rather scarce in the days when fires were generally of wood or peat. The rubble filling of walls is often more like a rubbish dump, fragments of broken pots and rubbish of all kinds being mixed in.

The doors and windows gave the mason scope for some invididual work, and these show most variation in detail, while adhering closely to a common form. The door jambs in all the seventeenth century houses are compound, usually built up of several separate stones, alternately long verticals and shorter horizontal binders which tie a long way into the wall, each side of the door. The lintel is a single stone, carved with date and initials, or just chamfered out on the under edge, with simple mouldings carried down the jambs to a plinth near the floor level. In the earlier houses it is general to keep these mouldings simple, and close to the door opening, but later, after about 1650, the moulding is carried up into the pattern of the date carving and becomes fairly elaborate. The date stone has the initials of the owner and his wife, usually arranged with the surname initial above and the two Christian name initials below. A few examples add the initials of the builder or master mason, e.g. at Arncliffe, a stone has the following arrangement

R.L.C.

1632   H.B.

L. and C.R. being owners, and H.B. the builder.

If the date stones are studied by broad districts as well as chronologically, it is soon evident that there are definite local fashions and traditions. On the whole, those of Upper Wharfedale are the simplest, usually a date and initials in sunk rectangles, on a stone that is plain except for the top moulding of the door opening, carried across its lower edge. There is sometimes a very flat arch, either three centred or of two straight limbs. In Wensleydale the top mould of the door rises in two curved or rectangular extensions into the door head, and initials and dates are carved on the flats between or at the side of them. In the later examples there are often three such insets of moulding, the middle one

---

* e.g. "J.P. the stone cutter, for a cornice 40 ft. long, cut and squared stones, at 18d. the foot."

much higher than the side ones. Ribblesdale has the most elaborate, with two or three inset mouldings, often elaborated by lateral lobes, not always in very good taste, the initials most commonly cut in separate recesses for each letter. In the latter part of the seventeenth century there is a tendency for over-elaboration of this type of date stone, and towards the use of smaller rectangular tablets inset in the wall, above a plain headstone. It is not wise, however, to generalise except when sufficient illustrations can be printed for discussion, and it would then be difficult to make choice among the many hundred examples drawn.

The mullioned windows conform very closely to one set of proportions, and are admirably designed to admit the maximum of light. The opening is deeply splayed, with simple mouldings outside, the mullions are diamond section, and the inside openings both over and at the sides are also widely splayed. The result is that the sun can shine in through a very wide angle, although the actual glass pane is rather narrow. In a great many measured examples the effective window angle is 120 degrees, that is, the sun shines directly into the room, between 8 a.m. and 4 p.m. true time if the room faces south. With the common addition of a west window to the parlour that room has sun all day. The inside cill of the window is nearly always cut out as a window seat, and as walls are commonly 2 feet or 2 feet 6 inches thick, with the window glazing 9 inches from the outside, this is wide enough to be very comfortable. Window openings are protected by a hood moulding carried over and turned down about 12 inches at each end, with a short horizontal return or finial, or in later buildings made continuous as a string course round the whole building, rising over each window and door. The hood moulding is usually convex above with a deep concave hollow mould on the underside to secure a free drip, and the deep shadow it casts, makes an essential feature in the aspect of the building.

The principal door may be elaborated by a porch, and this feature gives play to great individuality. The porch entrance is deep and open, with stone seats on each side, inside, with the door still in the main wall of the house. Above the porch an extra room is secured and this usually has more window than other rooms, the full front and part of the sides being opened, forming a fine look-out if used as a small retiring room by the lady of the house. In a few cases the upper part of the porch is used as a pigeon loft, with lighting boards of stone making a decorative feature, as at Town Head, Malham, etc. The porch roof makes a gable at right angles to the main roof.

Roofs are timbered with oak, and from the frequency of the use of whole section trunks only roughly dressed with an adze and with much of the bark still on them, it seems clear that there was little timber large enough to get sawn beams without import from other areas. The common roof truss is simple, king post purlins are usually quartered trunks, and spars are often roughly split thinner branches. The laths for the slates are also "splits" and one often comes across small items such as "J. Scott, cleaving the laths, 4/2," or "for cleaved laths and spars, 8/-." In most cases a roofer or slater was employed by the owner of the house, separate from the mason, and typical charges are "Robt. Kirkby, slater, roofing 2 rods 5½ yards, 7 yards to the rod, @ 11/- the rod," and "Robt. Grey, slating the house, 22 days at 16d. the day, getting the stones at 12d. the day, his labourer at 6d. the day." The roofing slates are thin flagstones, mostly got from two sources, either the beds near the base of the Millstone Grit, which gives a very heavy, coarse, well coloured and rippled

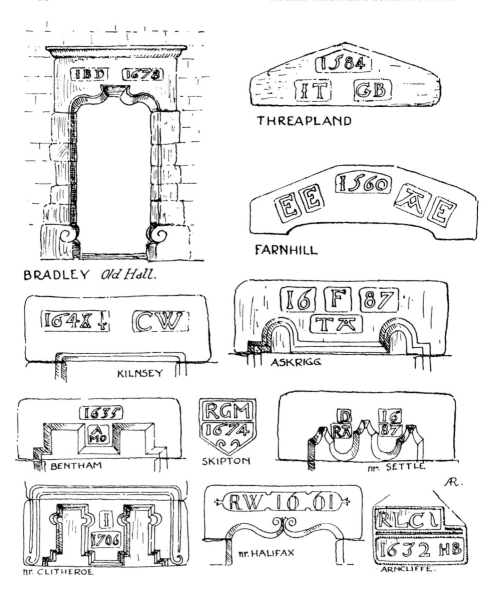

flagstone, not much more than 2 feet square, or from the flags below and above the Simonstone limestone. These latter were quarried extensively near Hawes, Askrigg and Carperby in Wensleydale, near Low Row in Swaledale, and near Beckermonds in Langstrothdale. A few localities in Coverdale supplied much of mid-Wharfedale with flags from the same horizon. Millstone Grit flags were quarried on Mallerstang Edge, near Keld, and on Fountains Fell. The "Hawes" flags are finer grained, smooth, and thinner, and are used in larger sizes sometimes reaching 4 feet by 3 feet for eaves courses. The ridge of the roof is covered with wide V-shaped ridges cut from the coarse Millstone Grit used for door and window openings.

The gable ends of the roof are finished in most cases by a course of coping stones laid over the ends of the roof slates, coming from a finial stone on the ridge end, or base of a chimney, down to a corbel at the eaves level. The ridge end may be finished with a stone ball or more elaborate finial, and a similar ornament is sometimes placed on the coping corbel. Properties that have belonged to religious orders like the Knights of St. John of Jerusalem have stone "lanterns" or cross finials on the corbels, and good examples of these can be seen in many parts of the Dales, e.g., Harden Beckfoot, near Bingley, Shipley Low Hall, etc. In the Glusburn-Cowling area there are two or three buildings in which the stone finial is replaced by a wrought iron cross, as at Glusburn Corn Mill, again the sign of one of the religious orders.

Chimneys are made with well cut stones laid on edge, with a small plinth base and a projecting, slightly moulded string course just below the top, giving the chimney an appearance of finer finish than is seen on most of the rest of the house. The chimneys are practically always on the ridge of the roof and, if at a gable end, the whole chimney structure from ground level may be built up as a narrowing projection, or in the upper part it may be carried out from the general gable face on a row of stone corbels, either arrangement giving a very pleasing break to the dull surface of the gable.

In the districts south of Airedale, where the general mass of the country is of coal measure rocks, the buildings have better finish, due to the use of many fine quality free-stones and flagstones of that formation. It is quite common to find a whole house front built with cut and shaped stone where in the northerly Dales would be used rough boulder walling. In the cut stone area walls can be made thinner, and details of moulding, doors and windows more finely tooled. Even with the change of material and dressing, however, the general plan and all the features so far discussed remain the same, true to the common tradition.

The type of house so far discussed is usually the homestead of a farm, and has associated with it farm buildings, either adjacent to it, or on the fringes of the village, but as these are often of somewhat earlier date, they will be dealt with later, along with smaller halls of sixteenth century date.

3. Smaller Halls

Most villages in the Dales possess both "Manor House" and "Old Hall", names which indicate a prime difference of function and may accompany a marked difference in structure of the two buildings. The names themselves are often of fairly recent origin and really come into common use only after the enclosures.

The distribution of manors and villages at the Norman Conquest was made on a lavish scale, favoured individuals becoming owners of scores of manors, as in the case of Osbern de Arches who was given 67 manors in the West Riding, or Roger of Poictou who held 45 manors in Craven alone, with the inevitable result that after frequent sub-infeudations or sub-letting, many manors were held in farm by a sub-tenant, but owned by an absentee lord of the manor. The sub-tenant, usually a member of a land-owning family, built himself a house or "hall" of residence, occupied by himself or his nominee, while the lord of the manor built a house and farm for the occupation of his steward who was the principal officer of the manor, and who also farmed or supervised the manorial portions of the common fields and wastes. The hall in time became the

Gateway, Kildwick Hall   D. Binns

residence of a wealthy family for generations, becoming the largest house in the village and called the hall, and later the "old" hall, while the manor house often remained only a better class farm, occupied by the steward of the manor, appointed from outside, changing its tenant frequently and never becoming the ancestral home of one family.

Some of the manors were very large, including many villages, e.g., the manor of Giggleswick included Stainforth, Rathmell, Kirkby Malhamdale and Litton as Bailiwicks (part of a manor managed by a bailiff), while other manors were much smaller than the area of a single township, e.g., Grassington had two manors while Broughton had four. It frequently happened therefore that a village acquired more than one hall or more than one manor house, though the latter is a rare case.

The "hall" was generally a timber structure and, if we are to rely on the few available descriptions, was little more than one large room with possibly a small lean-to withdrawing room until the fifteenth century when a more ambitious plan became customary and remained as the nucleus of the later "hall" which is the subject of this study.

In the sixteenth century the "hall" had become the typical residence of the wealthier yeoman farmer and of the clothiers who were becoming prosperous and, in common with the smaller houses already described, the hall was generally rebuilt in stone, or extended, to keep pace with the increasing wealth and importance of its tenant family. Many fine examples date from the latter half of the sixteenth century but in general the halls we know in the Dales were built in stone in the middle years of the seventeenth century when wealth had been reinforced by marriage into the smaller county families. In some cases the hall is merely a reconditioning in stone of an earlier timber building, or it includes in its principal rooms part of the structure of the earlier house.

The essential plan of the fifteenth and sixteenth century hall is fairly simple, admirably suited to its duties, capable of very little useful variation except in detail. The centre of the house is the hall, called the "house place" or "house body," with kitchen and parlour opening from it at two opposite ends, giving an approximate H plan. The house place is a large square, or nearly square, room, very high, making an imposing and well proportioned apartment, open to a timber roof. The main door, with or without a porch, opens at one corner of this room, on the south front of the house, directly into a through passage crossing one end of the house place, to a back porch or door in the north wall. This passage is separated from the hall by screens, usually of carved oak, standing only part of the height of the room, and carrying the gallery that in many cases is wrongly called the "minstrels' gallery."

The gallery may traverse two sides of the hall, giving access to the first floor rooms above the kitchens and parlour.

The south wall of the hall is largely occupied by a window, often the glory of the house, with a large fireplace on the north wall, or opposite the screen. The kitchens usually open from the screens passage, and the parlour from the opposite side of the hall, but these arrangements are varied in many ways in the different buildings. A staircase to the gallery and the first floor rooms may be included in the hall, but a common sixteenth century practice was to build the stairs in a small separate room, making them rise in short straight flights separated by landings, around the sides of a square well. Such a staircase is beautifully preserved in Kildwick Grange. Before the introduction of this fashion nearly all staircases were stone built in the thickness of the wall, and of the newel (circular) type.

The large window is the most striking external feature of the hall, as it is nearly twice the height of the other windows, often seven, eight, nine, or even twelve lights wide, with one or two transoms dividing it into two or three horizontal tiers of light. The window is covered with elaborate hood-moulding, or by the trimmed eaves of the hall, the mullions and transoms are well moulded and finely tooled. It is fairly common to find one or two panes of old glass, with initials, arms, or a date of the building period.

The chimney breast is large, occupying a good part of one wall of the room, usually a large ingle in which there was a free standing iron "range" or fire basket, with iron "dogs" for use when large logs were burnt. The chimney may project beyond the wall, if on an outside wall, giving very great depth to the ingle without standing too far out into the room. The arch of the ingle is usually inherited from the best Tudor traditions, a flat arch, with two flat limbs grading into the jambs through a circular curve, or a depressed three- or four-centred arch, well moulded. Armorial bearings are sometimes carved on the chimney mantel. The chimneys have a wide straight flue, where possible, bent flues becoming common only in a later period. The furnishings of the hall are fairly simple, a large table under the window of the type called "refectory table", a few chairs and stools, forms at the table, and one or two chests, placed along the screens.

The furnishings are specified in many contemporary inventories and wills and there is a striking uniformity in such lists, both over a wide area and for a century of time, which suggests that furnishing and the household life that used them were very much the subject of traditional fashion.

The inventory of her household goods made by Judith Nettleton in 1707 is typical of many. She lived at Ryecroft Hall, Tong, a house largely rebuilt in 1669, of the usual plan, a large central hall with screens and parlour to one side and kitchens behind, a great chamber over the parlour and smaller rooms over kitchen and buttery.

"In the house body
long table, 2 ferms and a wood banke	15	0
6 seeled chares and two throwne chares	11	0
one litell tabell and fower stowells	1	6
one iron drping pann	5	0
one range	12	0
two spits and iorne rakes	4	6
one iorne fire shoule, two pare of tonges, one iorne fire poite and striking bill and 2 choping bills, one iorne jacke and smoothing iorne	4	3
two brace ladells and a brace candlestick	1	0
one brace pott and a litell brace pann and one iorne pan	6	0
five sowed quishing and 3 sett quishings	2	8
one backon flicke and 5 befe flicks	17	0

In this list there are a few items only that need comment, to help us form a clear picture of the room. Ferms are the wood forms on each side of the large table, and the wood bancke is a form with solid back, later called a long settle, probably standing in one side of the large chimney opening. Seeled chares are chairs with a solid wood seat and back, and throwne chares have legs and back made of turned wood spars. The sowed quishings would be the loose and embroidered cushions used on the seeled chares, and the sett quishings are upholstered chair seats, probably on the two throwne chares and a stool.

Stowells are, of course, stools, while "fire poite" persists with us in the dialect "fire pote" often used for poker. Striking bill is a hooked implement for adjusting and moving logs on the fire, and the choping bills are kept handy for trimming logs. The flitches of bacon and beef in the chimney or on the ceiling reminds us of a Yorkshire furnishing now almost vanished, but deeply mourned and respected. The range and all its fixtures are counted part of the furnishings, and until well into the eighteenth century they occur among the personal possessions bequeathed by will, usually from father to son.

The parlour, across the screens passage, was not only "my lady's chamber" and withdrawing room, but was also the principal bedroom, holding the best bed, and chests for clothes, and sometimes a cupboard for the pewter and silver. Judish Nettleton's parlour is like those of most of her contemporaries of similar standing.

> "In the parler –

one bed with bedding and a foote chest	2	0	0
a little turell (truckle) bed		2	0
a chist		3	0
a chist of drawers		12	0
a cupbord with sowed hinger		8	0
a meale arke		8	0
one other chist		6	0
one wood banke and a litell bord		2	0
fower seeled chares		6	0
one range and grate		3	0

The kitchen furniture was mainly the table, chests, "dresser" for pewter or wooden "pots", and cooking utensils, spits, pans, fire irons, cleaver and chopping block, mortar for herbs and wheat, etc. The smaller first floor rooms all have bed and chests and all spare space seems to have been used for storage of one kind or another. The buttery generally contained the large bowls used for creaming the milk, the cheese press, and pans and ladles used in cheese making; this room often served also as store and pantry. In Craven the buttery is generally supplied with substantial stone shelves of Horton Slate (brought from the old quarries near Helwith Bridge and Arco Wood, and used also for water tanks) with holes in which the milk bowls would stand.

An inventory of nearly a century earlier will fill out a few details and also emphasise the very slight change made in a century – the list belongs to a house in Spofforth parish, and is dated 1614 –

> "great halle – three tables, j cobbard v formes ij loose boardes j skrine (screen) j needle wrought chear iij set quyshons vj tapestry quyshons j pare of tables (trestle table) i fyre shovle i pare of tonges.
> grandome chamber – one bed steed with sarsnet covering & v curtins j down bed ij blanketts j green rugg j pare of sheets. j table j green velvet chear j stole j nild (needle) worke quishon j ould green carpett j curtin rodd & iij green curtains. j pare tongs j pare of bellowes & j fyre shovle."

A Pudsey house in 1681 contained the following –

> "In the House – j range and paire of tonges and fire Shovell two Jacks one fire
> pote and pare of Rakes and one spit one Iron pot and a pare of pots.
> One brasse pan three ladles one scimer one beefe fork and two prigs.
> One long table and two formes; two litle white *tables.
>
> Five chares and one dozen of quishings.
> One salt pye and one litle coffar, one brasse morter & an iron pestell two
> stooles one hour glasse and a landhorne.
> In the butterie – one glass case with eight pewter dishes one dozen and halfe of
> trenchers two pewter cans one candlesticke & poringer & two salts with a litle
> tin can.
> A brasse morter and pestell ten milke bowles one butter bowle five stone pots
> and flower (flour) pots."

It is not necessary to repeat these items for other rooms and houses, all follow a similar pattern and make it clear that there was very little difference in the furnishings from one place to another.

The typical 14th and 15th century plan can be seen, almost unaltered, in Nappa Hall, Wensleydale, Farnhill near Kildwick, Bolling Hall, Bradford, and many other halls, particularly in the Halifax district. The principal period of rebuilding was during the middle years of the 17th century; in most cases whilst the old plan influenced the building very materially, and details of windows, doors and fireplaces carried forward Elizabethan or Tudor traditions, many experiments were made towards a different front elevation. The old frontage of two gables with the recessed hall front between them was gradually replaced by a three gabled front; there was at the same time a definite move towards symmetry of masses and of detail. In the older buildings, asymmetry is the rule. Windows vary in size according to the use of the room and no attempt is made to match them up, many of them lie to one side of the middle line of a gable, and they may occur on very different levels along the same story. This entire lack of symmetry gives a piquancy to the elevations that is lost when all features become regimented in a perfect balance. The hall was now ceiled and a principal bedroom, or servants' bedrooms made over it, and with this the hall window was reduced in height to match the others.

The "lag" of styles in the Dales makes it very unsafe to generalise about the date of a particular house, as many windows and doorways that would be accepted almost anywhere as perfect examples of 16th century work, occur in buildings dated a century later. There was a marked conservatism in style; the builders displaced by the dissolution of the monasteries built their earlier halls in the best Elizabethan style and handed on details and plans to their apprentices who continued to build to this traditional pattern for two or three generations.

Slight differences are found in detail which can often give a broad hint of the general date, in the absence of a date stone. The mullions and transoms of early windows are almost always cut with a concave mould which at the beginning of the 17th century is replaced by a flat chamfer. After about 1630 it becomes increasingly common to make the mullions with a prominent convex or half round mould, and the same usually applies to the door jamb mouldings.

---

* The master and mistress of the house had meals at a "little table" in the chimney corner, while the rest of the household and servants dined at the long table and forms.

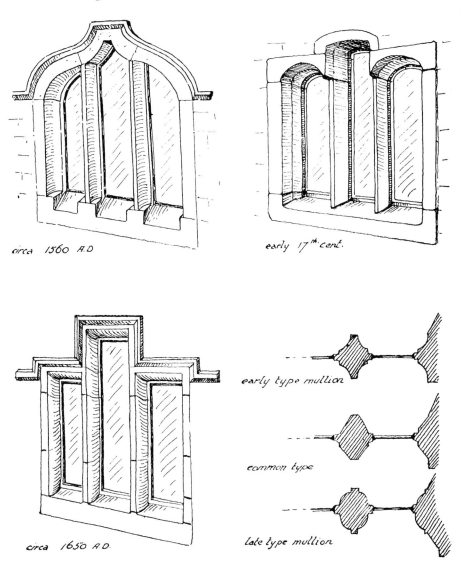

circa 1560 A.D

early 17th cent.

circa 1650 A.D

early type mullion

common type

late type mullion

Windows, except the hall window, are smaller in the early period and do not balance one another, but show every possible feature of asymmetry. The fireplace arches are built as a true arch made of many cut and shaped voussoirs, while after 1630 it is common to find the arch either made of 3 stones with "joggled" lines incised to give the appearance of many dovetailed stones, or to find it made of several "joggled" stones. Some of the earlier fireplaces are spanned by an oak beam which has a natural camber and is carried on oak jambs with a slight corbel at the top.

Often the most critical structures in determining the date of a doubtful building will be found in the roof. Early roofs, which may have been exposed to the open hall chamber, are beautiful in their lines and strength – later ones are built as a plain queen post or collar beam truss such as can be seen in most barns where the roof is meant to be unseen and take no part in the general design of the interior. The two illustrations are of early roofs and accompany hollow moulded mullions, Jacobean curved headed windows, and very early screens and panelling.

In many houses a porch has been added in the 17th century to a much older structure, as at Elslack Hall, where a porch and other "restorations" were made in 1672 on what is a 16th century building, with parts which may be older than that. In such cases only a close scrutiny of building details, the "keying in" of walls, alteration of roof levels seen on the gables, shifting of window positions, etc., can give one certainty of the general date. This critical examination of our Craven buildings will reveal a wealth of traditional stone craft and inventive genius far in excess of what most people will expect. A trained eye will always find greater joy in such a building, by reading in the stones a history not to be found in manuscript or printed books.

4. Farms

As previously mentioned, on many farms in the Dales the farm buildings, or part of them are frequently older than the dwelling house. While this is often true of the actual structure of the building, it is also essentially true of the traditional arrangement of the inside of the buildings, even of some where the structure may be as recent as the 19th century, and more so for the routine followed within them. The plan and arrangement of a typical Dales barn and shippon or laithe, the nomenclature of its parts, and the language of its occupations and routine come to us almost unchanged from our Anglo-Danish and Norse forebears. Some of the purest parts of our dialect are those associated with the farm, with sheep and cattle, and with all the varied incident of the farm year.

The houses and halls preserve some earlier traditions, but in their essentials they only date back into the 15th or 16th centuries; the farm buildings may in their structure date from the 15th or any later century, but they preserve clearly and with little modification the dimensions and adaptations that were becoming old at the time of the Norman Conquest. The agricultural system that was in operation during the 16th and 17th centuries was only a little changed from that introduced to the Dales by the immigrants arriving here in the 8th to 10th centuries.

The Anglian village had its small group of homes little better than hovels or mud huts, grouped round a central space that often later became a village green; near to them were a few buildings for the oxen, though many of the beasts shared house-room with the labourers. On the manor demesne, the land of the lord of the manor, there were barns and outbuildings for crops and cattle and stables for his horses. The village nucleus was surrounded by its common fields – the plough land close at hand, meadows near the river or lowland, the pasture and the waste lands beyond the common fields climbing to the fell tops. The ploughed land, two or three fields of a hundred acres or so each, was cultivated according to an unchanging rotation, wheat or rye in one field, oats or barley in another, and the third field fallow. The plough was built of wood shod with iron for coulter and share, and was the product of the village craftsman, smith and carpenter; it was drawn by a team of four or eight oxen. In an average village there might be three or four ploughs and as many as 30 or 40 oxen used for ploughing and all draught purposes where horses or tractors are used today. A few cows, a bull, and a fair number of sheep for wool and milk, and a miscellany of goats, pigs, geese and poultry made up the principal stock of the community.

It was one of the many services due from the peasant to his overlord, that he should care for and house the oxen, and one rank of tenant held his allotment of acres in the common fields in virtue of services which included, sometimes, the care of two oxen. The serf holding no property of his own, was stocked by the lord of the manor – for the carrying out of his services and for his maintenance – with 2 oxen, a cow, 6 sheep, and tools for his labour, and usually had only his own dwelling in which to house the oxen and cow.

It is not necessary to expand this discussion further at present, beyond emphasising that many of the Dales villagers, by the terms of their service or bondage, had to find house-room for two or more oxen. It was established at a very early period, even in Roman times, that two pairs of oxen for their standing room and to have turning room, needed a space of about 16 feet wide and a depth of about 8 to 10 feet. Palladius, a Roman architect writing in 210 A.D. says "eight feet are more than sufficient standing room for a pair of oxen, and 15 feet for the breadth of the oxhouse." These dimensions soon became the basic standard of the Anglian house and persisted for many centuries to influence building design.

The house structure was very simple – two pairs of "crucks" were made by selecting suitably bent oak trees, splitting them lengthwise and setting up the curved and trimmed beams so obtained, to form an almost "Gothic" arch or gable. The two gables were set up 16 feet apart, each with a cross piece set horizontally at about 6 or 8 feet from the ground, and projecting at each side of the "cruck" at least as far as the span of the feet. These A-shaped gables were connected by a ridge-tree from apex to apex, and by two horizontal ties laid on the ends of the cross pieces and called "pans". The "pans" later came to be called "wallplates", and made with the cross ties a rectangular frame for the room. The space between the legs of the crucks and from the ground level to the pans was filled in with wattle and clay daub, or with a more substantial wall of turf or stone, which at the gables was carried up to the apex. The roof with its very steep pitch and long slopes was thatched with rushes or heather. In 1454 in an account for Kirkby Malham parish there are several items similar to the following "paid for thakke bought of T. Rakys and watlyng and thekkyng 2 houses entirely viz: his said dwelling house in Ayrton and the barn of the said house, 18/4. Also for thekke bought and carriage to the barn of Tho. Paxton in Kirkby, 8/-."

The feet of the crucks were generally set on large stones for a firm footing, and in the same accounts we get the following item "Also at the erecting of the house of T. Paxton, 4d. Also for drink given to the carpenter and for basyng the said houses that is to say for laying great stones under the foot of the Crokk, 4d." Such a structure can be seen in a small barn at Bolton Peel, near Bolton-by-Bowland, where the crucks are set on a footing of large stones which project beyond the walls of the buildings and look, from outside, like small buttresses. The floors within these buildings were usually of beaten earth or cow dung mixed with clay, which made a good hard surface.

The upland farming of the Dales was strongly influenced by Norse as well as by Danish settlers, and a custom of both these peoples, that of having two types of houses – a summer-house and a winter-house – has left its mark on the area. The summer-house was a small cot or "sheiling" set up on the higher pastures and occupied by the cowherd and shepherd during the season that the cattle were fed in the open. It was constructed of light crucks and wattle, easily erected and easily moved. Such a place with the temporary pastures and other appurtences was known to the Norse people as a "Saeter" (Anglicised to *seat* or *sett*) and the name remains abundantly evident in our place names, e.g. Countersett, Buttersett, Woodseats, etc., and Summerlodge, Summerscales (*scales*, from old Norse *skali*, a shepherd's summer hut) Summersgill, etc.

The winter-house was a far more permanent structure established in or near the village and it commonly united in one structure the family house and the stalls where the cattle were kept and fed through the winter; this combined house and shippon was later called a "cote" or "coit" (old English *cot*) again a term well represented among local place names, e.g., Ulcote, Arncliffcote, Coldcotes, etc. It was the typical "cote" that was translated during the 16th and 17th centuries from a timber and thatch crucked building, into the long stone farmhouse of the Dales, which gave the pattern to which many of our farms conformed until a much later period.

Before discussing the combined house and barn, it will be best to consider the barn and shippon by itself. The barns vary considerably in size, but fall into two natural groupings; the smaller barns attached to most farms and small-holdings are structures of 3 or 4 bays at most, while in sharp contrast with them are the very large and elaborate structures usually attached to manorial houses or monastic estates, the "tithe" barns, usually magnificent buildings of many bays length, extended in width by aisles that often gives them something of the character of a church. Of these latter, many fine examples are well known to all dalesfolk, such as the one at Wigglesworth on the Ribble, Gunthwaite near Penistone, the two at Bolton Priory, the ones at Riddlesden Hall, near Keighley, and many others.

In speaking of the crucked house it was said that the simplest building was one with two crucks, enclosing a room that was 15 or 16 feet long. The width was determined by the span of the cruck feet; Henry Best in his "Farming Book", written in East Yorkshire in 1641, says in detailing the work of the thatchers, that crucks are generally either 15 or 16 feet, or 19 or 20 feet high, and from many measured examples agreeing with this, the corresponding span of the feet seems to be 12 or 15 feet. Such a room, about 16 feet by 12 or 15 feet, forms a "bay" and the house could be extended by adding one or more bays to the end and further extended by putting on an aisle at one side, or "outshutts" (lean-to extensions) at the sides or ends. The bay soon became an almost standard measure and buildings were described as being so many bays in size; e.g. in Harrison's Survey of the Manor of Sheffield, 1637, the greater part of the buildings in the assessment of property are given as follows "A Tenement with a Dwellinghouse of 2 Bayes, a Barne of 3 Bayes and a Outshutt", "a Dwelling-house of 4 Bayes" etc.

The bay of the timber and thatched building was usually 16 feet long and 12 to 15 feet wide, but when barns were built in the 16th century with a heavy stone slated roof, these spans were too great for safety with such great weight, and a common practice arose of setting the crucks or the roof principals only to

10 or 12 feet apart and making the barn 15 or 16 feet wide, so that the bay is generally 16 feet by 10 feet or 16 feet by 12 feet and a barn of 4 bays is about 40 to 50 feet long. Several barns can be found in any district where the change from a thatched roof to a stone roof is clearly seen, in the difference of the masonry added to the side walls to reach the eaves of the much flatter stone roof, and added at the corners to fill in between the old and new roof slopes. In nearly all cases when such alteration was made, the crucks were replaced by roof trusses, commonly a simple three member truss with two short diagonal braces. King post trusses were only generally introduced in the 18th and 19th century roof repairs.

The internal arrangement within such a barn was evolved during the Anglo-Danish period, and is still used with very little change. The first bay is generally used to house the oxen or cattle, putting four beasts in the width of 16 feet, giving them 7 feet or so head to tail, and allowing a cleaning alley behind them and against the end wall, in which there is the "muck hole" to the midden or "mixen". The cows stand in stalls separated by posts or partitions, the "skellboose" (old Norse; *Skille*, to separate and old English *bos*, old Norse *bass*, a stall); over the stalls is a floor, the "balks" on which part of the hay crop is stored. The second bay on to which the big doors of the barn open at one side, and on to which the cattle face, is flagged and forms the threshing floor. Opposite the big doors, which usually rise nearly the full height of the side wall, is a small door in the opposite wall, called from its ancient use, the "winnowing door". Corn was threshed on the flags with flails, and in windy weather was winnowed in the concentrated draught of the small door when the big doors were opened. The flags form a clean floor from which the cattle are fed, and a useful place for all sorts of odd jobs.

The third and fourth bays are the "mow" where the bulk of the hay is stored. Commonly there is a small "outshutt" or lean-to extension, built on the side of the bay against the large doors, used as a calf house, and continuing the normal roof slope. A wall on the opposite side of the doorway allows the roof to

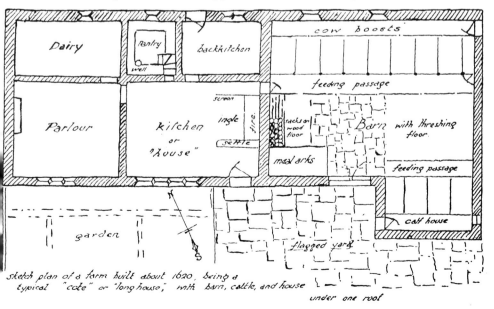

sketch plan of a farm built about 1620, being a typical "cote" or "long house," with barn, cattle, and house under one roof

be carried over the door as a useful porch. Often such a barn is called a "staggarth" or "Laithe", both names being of great antiquity – staggarth from O.N. *stakk*, stacks, and *gard*, a yard or enclosure; and the old Norse *hlatha*, a barn. These arrangements are identical, whether the barn be built on crucks at an early period, or built in stone in the 16th or some later century.

In some of the larger barns and in most of the tithe barns, the space is made much wider either by the addition of aisles or outshutts, and in these barns the cattle often stand in the aisles, facing into the central space or nave of the barn, and occupying two or even three bays, but not having any balks over them. It is not uncommon in both large and small barns to find at one end a bay that is arranged like a small house, with a narrow door and a window, with a floor at balk height, and often outside stairs to a chamber on the balks. It was often the custom to accommodate one or more farm labourers in the barn, both for living room and for protection for the cattle at night. In recent years, many people can remember the Irish labourers at hay time having shake-down beds on the balks. This use of part of the barn as a dwelling or sleeping place is indicated in many of the early wills, such as 1556 "In the oxen houses viij coverletts, iij blanketts, xiiis.iid." or 1569 "in the cowe house iij olde coverlets a paire of blanketts a paire of sheits a mattras and a bolstar."

Probably the combined dwelling and barn called a "cote" or "coit" is the most characteristic farm building of the dales, and a short description must now be given of its arrangement. It is essentially the "winter house" of the Norse settlers, and was very common all over the Pennines. The survey of Sheffield, 1637, has very many examples such as the following, "a Tenement called Tanfield with a dwellinghouse and a barne both under one roofe and also a croft," etc., and similar terms are met with in many deeds and land conveyances of the 16th and 17th centuries in the Dales. Another term that is sometimes used is "all that fyrehouse and barn" or "that dwelling house or fyre-house and barne" (Airton & Scosthrop deeds, 1625). This is the equivalent of the Norse term "eld-hus" literally fire-house (*eld*, fire, preserved in the dialect word *eldin*, firewood) and is used to differentiate that part of the building where the fireplace is situated, and the family live.

The plan is of a typical cote, still in occupation and little changed beyond the conversion of the doorway between the side of the fireplace and the feeding passage of the boose, into a cupboard. In the cote it was possible for the farmer to pass under cover around his stock, to keep watch and care over them at all times, and this was a decided comfort and advantage in some of the severe blizzards and snow storms that the higher dales have often experienced. The arrangement of the cote varies a little and its section is usually made asymmetric by outshutts for calf houses, dog kennels, and other small buildings. The cote is generally wider than an ordinary barn by the addition of one aisle at the back, and this is occupied in the barn partly by the cows, and in the house part accommodates dairy and pantry. The roof comes down much lower this side than at the front. The large barn doors give on to the threshing floor, and there are usually one or two small doors in the end wall, from the cow booses and calf hull on to the yard. In barns, both large and small, it is not uncommon to find pigeon "cotes" built into the end wall, generally over the house part. The pigeons were an essential source of fresh meat during the winter season. Before the introduction of turnips and winter feed for cattle in the 17th century, all stock not required for breeding in the next year and for replenishing the herds was killed off and salted down by Martinmas (Nov. 14) and during a few months when that was the only meat available, fresh pigeons were welcome.

There is a fine 16th century barn in Grassington in which an outshutt on one side of the large doors, one bay wide, is carried up to roof level, and forms a dog house below, and a columbarium or dove house in the upper part. Here there are well-built nesting holes in all walls with a small door by which the place can be entered from a ladder. In many cases the pigeons occupied a loft over the upper room of the house bay.

In looking at these old barns, it will often be seen that only local short and twisted oak scrub had been used for roof spars, small trunks split and quartered, reaching only from one purlin to the next and not, as nowadays, from eaves to ridge tree. The tie beams of the roof trusses are often carried on a stone corbel, and in a few cases this has been tooled by the mason into simple moulding. The principals are pegged together and members tenoned into one another. The trusses were evidently assembled in position, as most examples are marked at every joint with cleanly scribed Roman numerals to assure the proper assembling. There is good evidence that the tie beam was first got into place and secured in the wall top before the rafters were erected. These have a butt joint together, well pegged, and the ridge tree rests on a small flatted top or is slightly sunk into them. It is rare in the early roofs to find the rafters butting on to the ridge.

In the larger barns with aisles the roof trusses are carried on massive oak pillars with a longitudinal beam where the wall plate would have been. The span is usually increased so that the central nave is about 20 ft. wide and the aisles from 10 to 15 ft., the tie beams being about 20 ft. from the floor. In these larger span trusses a king-post is fairly common. The fine timber work is one of the most attractive features of these barns.

Few of the barns preserve their old furniture but on rare occasions a flail or a winnowing fan are to be found among junk stored on the balks. The meal arks that often stood at the back of the threshing floor are still sometimes seen, and some people still remember in their boyhood the times spent stamping down oatmeal with their feet to pack it tight and solid in the ark so as to keep for the whole year. For many a cote and barn the oldest road is that to the manor mill, by which the grain was taken from the threshing floor to be ground and brought back as meal to be stored in the arks; these old "mill roads" are often mentioned as ancient rights in leases and sales of farms.

Most of the old barns covered by this article lie near or adjoining a farm house or a village. There are many similar small isolated laithes and shippons scattered in the fields up most of the dales that conform to the plan here described in almost every detail, but which were built about the end of the 18th century when the fields were enclosed. Some of the scattered laithes, however, are older and the enclosure fields were fitted to meet them, but each example must be studied with care if far from farm or village, and in making an estimate of its age one must remember the continuity of tradition and plan with little fundamental change for a thousand years.

During the 16th and 17th centuries, most of the cotes and farms were occupied by small yeomen or yeoman farmers who combined their arable land with a few sheep and cows; they produced bread and beer from their own oats and barley, meat, milk and cheese from their cows and meat and wool from the sheep. Wool was carded and spun in the farmhouse and either sold to the travelling packman who collected for the weavers, or woven at home. The stock of such a farm was small when compared with one of today; there are abundant details to be read in contemporary wills and inventories of which the following is entirely typical:

> 1599. John Hudson, yeoman farmer: "4 kyne, 2 stotts, one boyle stirke, 3 calves, one mare, 24 shepe, corn & hay in the barne, 1 cock & 5 hens"; or 1611, Thos. Slater left "54 ewes, lambs, hogges & twinters, 4 heffers, 1 horse and a twinter coult, 4 kyne & 6 calves."

A fair general average, based on about fifty wills, etc., works out at 5 cows, 2 to 5 oxen, 20 to 40 sheep and a horse. Nearly all such wills include a spinning wheel or two, a store of wool or yarn, and occasionally a loom and its accessories.

Standing in one of these old laithes there is a sense of peace and a timeless atmosphere not often found outside. The slow, gentle life of cattle, the bringing in of crops, good or bad, and the work associated with them, has gone on its quiet unhurried way for many centuries, and few places are still so unchanged and even yet unchanging as the old-fashioned laithe or shippon of our Dales. In these buildings man has disciplined himself and his activities to accept the rule of the seasons, to place his faith in the inevitableness of seedtime and harvest, and to serve his stock, recognising their entire dependence on his care.

The outside world of political and social change seems far off and of little permanence when viewed from the world of the barn and shippon, and it is to be hoped that with the revival of agriculture now taking place, with its introduction of motor tractors, milking machines, and hygienic buildings, we manage to preserve not only a few of the older houses, but all of the peace and stability they represent.

5. Schools

Yorkshire has for many generations prided itself on a wealth of soundly established and well-endowed grammar schools, not all of them in the larger cities, but some found in the smaller market towns and even in the remoter dales villages. The 16th and 17th centuries were marked by the foundation of a great number of these schools and of some that have since ceased to rank as grammar schools or have entirely disappeared. It is the purpose of this article to describe briefly the few school buildings of that period which remain and to sketch in a few details of their historical background, and the life lived in them. In our county there are at least three schools of pre-Norman date of foundation, those attached to the Saxon ministers of Beverley, York, and Ripon; these schools were almost entirely limited to the training of young boys who were to enter the monastery as monks and the subjects taught are strictly related to the life and service of the monastery.

During the earlier years of the monastic houses, say the 12th to the 14th centuries, it was usual for wealthy persons to seek to promote the spiritual welfare of themselves and others by the endowment of "chantries" within the monasteries or at a parish church, and as many of our older schools originated as "chantry schools" it will be useful to make clear the relation of the chantries and chantry schools to the later "grammar school".

The essential idea of a chantry benefaction was the gift of an endowment, either for a specified period or in perpetuity, which would be sufficient to pay for the services of a priest or monk to say Masses and prayers for the donor's spiritual welfare while alive, and for his quick release from Purgatory after death. This service of prayers was said daily in the course of the monastic services, and took its proper place in the long list of prayers for benefactions and Masses said for particular persons, but the duty was performed by the community of the monastery in general with their other duties. Some of the more zealous individuals soon preferred that the intercession for their welfare should be the especial function of one particular priest, rather than part of the general duties of all, and to meet this desire "chantries" were founded, either within or independent of the monastic community.

The Masses were to be said at a particular altar named in the endowment, or occasionally a new altar would be erected within a church or in a chapel added to an existing church. During the 13th century as monastic orders were seen to be relaxing something of their earlier discipline and simplicity of life, the custom of founding chantries outside the monasteries rapidly increased. The name arose from the singing of the Mass on special days, and the fact that chantry priests attached to the altar of a parish church or collegiate church gave help in the choir services as a singer. As the duties of a chantry priest did not include any parochial work and the priest was in no sense a curate even if attached to a parish church, he was a man of comparative leisure between the official hours of his services, and this free time was often made of use to the community by employing him as a schoolmaster. The chantry priests were drawn from the fairly large body of unbeneficed priests that was typical of the period.

In some cases the endowment of a chantry included the provision that the priest should teach local children, as for example, at Well, where the chantry priest was also by licence, "a scholemaster of a free grammar schole for the better bringing up and instructying of children" and was paid for this service £6:13:0 yearly, and at Gargrave, where in the Chantry of our Lady there was "one preist founde by the parochiners there, as well to teache theyre children as to assist the vicar in serving the cure."

The chantries were finally abolished after a survey of them, made by commissioners appointed under Acts of Henry VIII and Edward VI in 1545 and 1547, but in many where the priest also performed schoolmaster duties the endowment was altered in such a way as to become the endowment of a school, and to continue the work of education. It must be remembered that Henry VIII, whatever his later character, was an unusually well educated man for his period and had a real interest in education. At the dissolution of the monasteries it was his desire and intention to establish schools on a wide basis. His scheme included the establishment of a Bishop of Fountains to rule Lancashire and West Yorkshire, with his seat at Fountains Abbey, assisted by a dean, six prebendaries, six minor canons, and masters of grammar schools and song schools (Letters Patient, xiv (2) pp 428-30) to serve all the area, but the pressure of foreign trouble turned the available funds to army expansion, and education was defeated as on most occasions since then.

In spite of the failure of the larger schemes, great encouragement was given to the extension of schools by the continuation of the chantry school endowments; some of these schools were re-endowed during the reign of Elizabeth or of Charles I, and in some cases were given a charter of foundation as a royal grammar school. In most cases this second endowment period saw the first attempt to provide a proper school building, the chantry schools being held either in the priest's house or in many cases in the porch of the parish church. During the 17th century in addition to the expanded chantry schools many "grammar schools" were built and endowed in towns and villages by successful citizens who made fortunes in the expanding trade and markets of the time.

The chantry schools of the dales area include Skipton (later Ermysted's) Grammar School, Giggleswick School, and Sedbergh School, all expanded beyond recognition, and three or four that have entirely disappeared, among which are Kirkby Malham, Richmond, Gargrave and Long Preston. The schools founded by successful citizens include Burnsall, Threshfield, Bingley, Slaidburn, Otley and many others. Buildings of the period we are discussing in this series of articles, remain at only a few of the schools, Otley, Ilkley, Burnsall, Threshfield, Skipton and Slaidburn (1717) and Sedbergh (1716) just at the end of the period, but these are sufficient to give some idea of plan and arrangement and to allow the formation of some picture of life in these early schools that will be related to actuality.

Skipton Grammar School will afford an example of the transition from chantry to a fully fledged school. The report of the Chantry Commission in 1545 mentions four chantries in Skipton, of which one is "the chauntrie of Saynt Nicholas in the saide churche" – St. Nicholas was the patron saint of learned clerks and schoolboys – "Stephen Elys incumbent, Havying no foundation as he allegyth, but by report one Peter Toller, clerke, founded the same, to th' extent to pray for hys sowle . . . and also to keep a grammar skole to the children of the same towne." The report of the second commission says "the Chaunty of Saynt Nicholas used as a free grammer schole in the Paryshe Churche there, Stephen Elys, incumbent and scholaster 42 yeres of age, a good grammaryan having scollers to the number of 120 & hath kept schole there these fyve yeres past." Toller was rector of one medeity of Linton and also Dean of Craven, died 1492 and buried at Linton, and so the school pre-dates 1492 in foundation.

In 1548 William Ermysted, Master of the Temple, founded a Grammar School in Skipton and his endowment of land and income was added to that of the existing chantry and the two merged in the new Grammar School. Ermysted made certain requirements clear in his deed of foundation from which we glimpse something of the school life. School was held in the building purchased by him from the Earl of Cumberland for the purpose, and is either the present "old grammar school" near the end of Newmarket Street, or a building on the same site. Boys were to be instructed in "Grammar Tongue" and were to be taught from 6 am to 11 am and 1 pm to 6 pm., between the 1st of March and the 1st of October, and during winter to start at 7 am and finish at 5 or 6 pm. The masters are "to inform the boys the Alphabet after a laudable Pronunciation of Syllables and afterward in the Art of Grammar and the Rudiments of the same to proceed well with the frequent use of the Latin Tongue" – more advanced boys were to compose "Epistles, Orations, Verses" and to study Virgil, Terence, Ovid and other authors. School should open and close with specified prayers, collect, and sung anthems.

At Giggleswick, the chantry of the Rood in the Parish Church, was founded by James Carr at the end of the 15th century, and in 1507 he had become sufficiently interested in the teaching in this chantry school, to secure a lease of land near the churchyard, and build a schoolhouse. In 1553 the chantry school having proved invaluable to the district, Edward VI granted a new charter transforming it to a Grammar School. The original building remained in use until its replacement by a larger one in 1797, and was a small two story building with outside stone stairs to the upper room. There was a small oriel window in the upper room and the rest of the windows on both floors were typical mullioned windows of the district. Reading was taught downstairs and writing upstairs. Like most schools of the time, the teaching was largely Latin and Divinity, with some singing. The masters are instructed to use no language but Latin in speaking to the scholars, wherever possible, and to the more advanced to use Latin, Greek and Hebrew.

Kirkby Malham had a similar school in the chantry of the Rood in the second bay from the east of the south aisle of the church, which was later endowed as a grammar school by Benjamin Lambert, and established in its own separate building. The story of many of the chantries is the same, the chantry endowment being absorbed in a new gift and a foundation charter being granted for a Free Grammar School.

Not many of the original buildings are left, but those that do survive conform to a very simple plan. Burnsall School was founded by Sir William Craven in 1602, and was particularly fortunate in the generosity of its founder and the fine building he provided. The school consists of school house for the master at one end, occupying two bays, then a well designed porch leading at one side into the school house (though this has also a separate door) and at the other into a schoolroom of three bays. The building is two storied, the room above the schoolroom being used at one time as a dormitory. The facade has two ranges of mullioned windows, the higher windows just under the eaves, and the ground floor windows just under a prominent moulded string course. The porch has a slightly pointed-arched entrance with deep mouldings, set in a rectangular mound that reaches to the string course; over the centre of the arch is a tablet set between classical columns bearing the inscription of the founder. All details of the building are such as we have seen in the best of the dales houses and smaller halls – the mullioned windows are mostly of four lights with well moulded framing; the porch and gables carry finial ornaments and on the eastern gable is a small belfry with the school bell. The chimneys at the junction of school and house are well designed in a stack with two shafts set diagonally on a plinth, and with deeply moulded cornices.

Threshfield Grammar School, now like Burnsall used as an elementary school, is somewhat simpler. It consists of a long schoolroom with two tiers of windows, three on the ground level and two above, on the main front, with two windows in the east gable. The porch is at the west end of the front, with a round shallow arch doorway, and above it a delightful three-light mullioned window lighting a small room which was provided for the usher's quarters. The building at one time was two-storied like Giggleswick and a part of the upstairs was the master's house, but at some date the schoolroom was opened to the roof. The chimney is plainer than at Burnsall but is still very graceful in its rather severe lines. Ilkley old school building is the simplest and smallest of those which survive, being a single room with a door entering without porch at the middle of the south side, and a fireplace and short chimney at the south west corner. The master would live "out" in this case. Otley Grammar School was housed in 1607 in an imposing gabled building facing up the main street, ornamented by beautifully proportioned, mullioned bay windows, and with most unusually slender gable finials. Its internal arrangement of several rooms was equally uncommon.

In all the schools of the period there was very close association of school and church, seen in the site of the buildings. In the case of Dent Grammar School, which was built by the gifts and endowments of the local dalesmen before 1603 when James I gave its charter, it was built at the bottom of the churchyard which was used by its boys as their playground. Like nearly all the schools it was at first two storied, but the floor was removed at a later period. Giggleswick School and Burnsall School were both built on land adjoining the church yard, and Sedbergh and Slaidburn Schools both built at the beginning of the eighteenth century are in similar positions. These last mentioned schools are both built in the early "Georgian" or classical style, though Slaidburn retains a fine dales influence in its windows.

In these grammar schools the sons of the yeoman farmers and the wealthier people were taught, but few of the sons of the agricultural labourers were free to take advantage of the education offered, as they were busy from very early years about the fields and farms. Many of the endowments included scholarships to Oxford and Cambridge, and a goodly number of great men were sent up by them. The teaching consisted mainly of Latin grammar and literature, divinity, and sometimes, mathematics and penmanship as extras. In most schools the master was assisted by an usher who taught the younger children and kept discipline among them. The two rooms were used for the younger and older scholars, the younger working away at "the rudiments" of grammar and writing, and the older ones wrestling with the classics and divinity. The schoolmasters were usually in Orders and thus closely connected with the Church and its teaching. In some cases older scholars gave help with the younger boys. The instructions for Sedbergh Grammar School, in 1528, say that if the master is absent "one of hys Scolers sufficiently lernyd to teach hys Scolers" shall substitute for him, and that he "was to teche frely gramer, ... but shall not be bounde to teche nor cause no scoler to teche any other thyng but gramer to any children, except the frends of the sayd children wyll gyffe the scholmaster ... for theyr labour, as they can agree."

The remaining schools are worthy of careful study and preservation, as they represent, with a few Friends' Meeting Houses and Independent Chapels, the only *public* buildings bequeathed to us by the period that is so rich in domestic and farm building. No time spent in studying their structural details will be wasted or regretted.

(September 1941 – February 1942)

BARDEN TOWER:
Wharfedale Lodge of
the Cliffords

In the Yorkshire Dales the place name "Tower" is rare. We can think of only four old examples: Barden Tower, Norton Tower, Clifford's Tower and Mortham Tower. Of these four, Barden Tower and Norton Tower are ruins, Clifford's Tower is nothing more than traces of the foundations, and Mortham Tower, with the addition of later buildings, is an occupied house. Yet all these buildings have interesting histories and have given rise to legends and poems, so it might be pleaded that there is sufficient excuse for telling something of their story and condition.

Before the Norman Conquest and throughout the following centuries of feudal England, hunting the deer, the wild boar and some other animals was the constant sport of kings and nobles. Cnut, the Scandinavian king of England, had created many royal forests and a mass of "forest laws" are credited to him, though they may, in fact, be of later date.

In the North of England there were extensive forests, both royal and those called "chases" which were held from the king by a subject. Soon after the Conquest, when Robert de Romille was given the Honour of Skipton, a number of small forests or chases in Craven were either created or were continued from the pre-Conquest times – Crookrise, Elso, Barden and others. Some larger ones included Langstrath and Litton Forest, Gisburn Forest and Knaresborough Forest, with many more further north.

To administer and keep the forests required a large number of officials and servants, many of whom lived in or near the forest. In some cases a village was built for the occupation, such as Buckden for Langstrathdale, Bainbridge for Wensley Forest, and others. In the smaller forests there were generally a few "lodges", occupied not by the chief officials but by keepers and minor officers.

Sometimes one lodge was more important than the rest and the home or lodging of a senior official and the seat of the forest courts. In the forest of Barden, which covered much of Wharfedale from about Bolton Priory to the boundaries of Appletreewick, there were several lodges: Drebley, Barden, Laund, Gamelsworth, Holgill and Ungayne. Of these lodges Barden soon became the most important, and probably was built as a small tower, more dignified and more commodious for the forest courts than any of the others. It was suited also as a place for protection of the wild area, which certainly suffered from Scots raids on more than one occasion in the 14th century.

It is likely, though we shall never know for certain, that the forest officers were able to leave the other lodges and take refuge here, defending themselves from attack by the Scots. After these raids, to increase the value of the tower if further troublous times occurred, the tower was built or rebuilt in the form of a strong pele tower, a place capable of defence and giving shelter to men and horses. At the end of the next century it was extended and enlarged by Henry, the 10th Lord Clifford, but something of the older tower remains in the walls of the main part of the building.

Whitaker quotes an old document among the manuscripts at Bolton, which says that "Barden had all the officers of a forest, as Verdurer, Forester, Regarder, Agister and Woodward. Also a Swainmote Court, where the forest-laws were executed, and offenders punished accordingly. It was within no constabulary, had not muster rolls for service; the inhabitants being only subject to the power and authority of the Lord.

"The Kings and queens of this realm never claimed to appoint constables, or other officers, nor demanded any subsidy or other tax or imposition within the same. None were ever pressed out of this forest for the service of the kingdom, nor any provision required therein. The inhabitants were always a free people exempt from gaulds and assessments for the highways, bridges, etc., yet have always had contribution from the wapontake for their own bridge.

"This forest was in ancient times a parish of itself, until the dissolution of the abbies, that the lord purchased Bolton Abbey, and then for his own ease, being bound to find a curate at Bolton, he caused the tenants to repair thither to hear divine service, to christen their children, and bury their dead. The forest of Barden is also a privileged place and no arrest, but by the officer of the same, can be made within it. Neither could any dogs be kept within the said forest, but according to assize, and a ring kept for the trial of the same."

This can leave no doubt at all that Barden was subject to the forest laws and that Barden Tower was the principal lodge, although others had a greater money valuation in the survey of 1310 when Drebley, Gamelsworth and Holgill were all valued at twice or more the amount of Barden. This higher valuation arises because the other lodges had meadow land around them of greater extent, while Barden lodge in the heart of the forest was more concerned with administration than with any cultivation or feeding of beasts.

Of the officers above mentioned, the Verdurer had to look after the game and timber, and his office was one of importance. Usually the position was held by letters patent of the crown, or by paying a fee to the king for the office and all its perquisites. Similarly the Forester was an important person, usually of some rank and standing in the following of the king or chief lord.

The Regarder made a survey of the forest every three years, and reported any encroachments on the limits of the forest, assarts or clearings made without authority, examined the hedges and fences, and kept the list of owners of bows, arrows, and hounds, any of whom might be tempted to do a little poaching. The Agister controlled the pasturage of cattle, collected fees, and arranged for pigs to have "pannage" of the acorns in proper season. Finally the Woodward had the charge of all the timber in the forest.

Within the forest bounds there was a Woodmote, or preliminary court, held every forty days, from which offenders against forest law were sent to the Swainmote Court of freeholders. The Verdurers were the judges and twelve freeholders within the forest made the jury. This court could order fines in all petty cases, but more serious offenders were sent by them to the Justices in Eyre, which from time to time held courts in the forest.

With the Swainmote and Woodmote held at the lodge of the Verdurer at Barden Tower, its importance was secured for as long as the forest lasted. The profits of the courts at Barden, the fines levied on offenders, became a regular item of income to the Cliffords.

The next stage in the tower's history came when Henry, the 10th Lord Clifford (1485-1524) enlarged it and practically rebuilt it. The neighbouring

Barden Tower   Dennis Mallet

chapel and priest's house were built at this time. This tenth Lord Clifford was known as the Shepherd Lord, from the circumstances of his being brought up in Cumberland. He was studious and it was reputed that he studied alchemy and was a wizard, but the legend that the canons of Bolton Priory assisted him in these studies is entirely without foundation.

In 1510, while the Shepherd Lord was living in Barden Tower, in preference to Skipton Castle, accounts were kept. A few of them have survived and give a hint of the kind of life lived there. Among other matters there were a few repairs but these seem to be quite ordinary; payment to the locksmith, the tower top was mended with sods, three stone of iron were bought in Penrith, two masons received a small payment, and the largest item was for "palyng" or fencing part of the park of Barden.

Other items in the accounts are far from confirming the general picture that has been given of him as a studious recluse, shut off from the world. There are entries for the carriage of a tun of wine from York to Barden, a swan from Appleby, carriage of a wild boar and other stuff to Barden, salt fish from Hartlepool and items for green ginger and treacle, with other foods.

Music and entertainment were a part of the life and some payments are for strings for a fiddle, for a bagpipe, a livery jacket for young Long the Piper, payment for the minstrels, for drums and shawms, for players from Halifax on St. Thomas's day and to "the lord of misrule," the leader in many pleasant festivities.

In the time of the Shepherd Lord, the tower had become a regular dwelling for him, the functions as a forest lodge having declined and much of the forest being settled in small freeholds with hamlets growing up like Drebley. The lodges generally became large farms and land was "assarted" from the forest for their cattle and crops. After the death of the tenth lord, Barden was neglected, and only very rarely used as a dwelling, sometimes as a hunting lodge, and sometimes as a temporary residence.

Margaret Countess of Cumberland stayed here for a short time before the birth of her daughter, Anne, the great-granddaughter of the Shepherd Lord. The tower became ruinous and totally neglected and nothing like the former state, when the 10th Lord kept 40 servants there, occurred again. Anne, the Lady Anne Clifford of Skipton, Appleby and many other places, inherited the Clifford estates in 1605 and soon after this began the repairs of Skipton Castle (also ruined) and Barden Tower. To mark the repair she had a great inscription cut and placed over the doorway on the south side, and one of the self-imposed tasks of most visitors is to read this in its entirety.

> *This Barden Tower was repayred by the Ladie Anne Clifford Covnte*
> *sse Dowager of Pembroke Dorsett and Montgomerie Baronesse*
> *Clifford Westomerland and Vessie Lady of the Honour of Skipton in*
> *Craven and High Sherifesse by inheritance of the Covntie of*
> *Westmerland in the yeares 1658 and 1659 after itt had layne rvinous*
> *ever since about 1589 when her mother then ley in itt and was greate*
> *with child with her till nowe that itt was repayred by the said Lady.*
> *Isa. Chapt. 58 ver 12 Gods name be praised.*

Three years earlier than this she had restored the Park of Barden and walled it in. She frequently stayed in the repaired tower, spending much of the summer time there, staying in Skipton or Appleby in winter. She slept at the tower for the first time in May 1659. She had six castles – Skipton, Barden

Tower, Pendragon (which she repaired in 1660), Brough, Brougham and Appleby – and she travelled between them on many occasions and often by different routes.

In 1662 she came from Appleby and on September 25th came "into the Inn at Settle, where I lay the night and never lay there before, and the next day, being the 26th, I came over the moor by Mawham water Tarne, where I had not been 9 or 10 years before, and so into my house at Barden Towers."

The notes of journeys in her diary are sometimes of great interest, as on October 6th, 1663, "After I had lain in Skipton Castle in ye chamber there wherein I was born, just 5 months from my coming from Barden Tower, did I remove thence onwards on my journey towards Westmorland, so I went to Mr. Cuthbert Wade's house at Kilnsey, and lay there ye night, and so ye next day from them through Kettlewell Dale, up Buckden Rakes, and over ye Stake into Wensleydale to my cosen Mr. Thos. Metcalfe's house at Nappa, where I lay also ye night, and on to Pendragon. And this was the first time I was ever in Kettlewell Dale or went over Buckden Rakes or the Stake or Cotter, or any of those dangerous places wherein yet God was pleased to preserve me on this journey."

Generally she was carried in a horse litter with some of her chief servants in a large coach. The rest of the numerous retainers rode horseback. On one journey she stayed the night at John Symondson's house in Starbotton, and on another occasion "I went to the Chappel of Mallerstang by the way for a while, it being the first time I was ever in the Chappel, and so over Cotter and dangerous ways into one Mr. Coleby's house near Bainbridge in Wensleydale, where I lay the night with my women servants and three of my men servants and my other servants lying at Askrigg and Bainbridge, and on to Kilnsey on the 17th."

After the death of Anne her son George stayed from time to time at Barden Tower, with his wife Lady Margaret, but from 1598 to 1605 it had been leased to a distant relative. It was not again leased or occupied in this way. After the death of Lady Anne, the property of the house of Skipton was divided and Barden descended with Bolton, through the Earls of Cork and Burlington to the family of the Dukes of Devonshire.

In 1745 among the documents relating to preparation to meet the Jacobite rebellion, it was noted that at Barden Tower there were 45 officers' pikes and staffs, 30 halberts, 30 drums and 48 drumsticks, enough to lead a considerable number of tenants if they were called out. The halberts and pikes still to be seen at the Tower are more likely to be part of these stores than to be, as is sometimes said, part of the equipment of Flodden Field.

In 1774 Whitaker saw the Tower complete, but later the lead and timbers of the roof were taken off and the building fell into general disrepair. In 1899 the outer walls were given some repair to make them safe for the visitors who were beginning to visit the site in increasing numbers. Because of the unsafe conditions of the walls, visitors can now only wander round the outside of the walls. However, a close look at the walls will soon reveal a complex history – patches and alterations can be recognised and the central part is seen to be really the older square tower of the Shepherd Lord, with Tudor alterations of windows and with additions particularly at the east end.

The "restoration" of Lady Anne Clifford was fairly drastic if one might judge from the contract for the work.

> June 2, 1657 Articles of agreement between the Right Hon. Anne countesse dowager of Pembroke, etc., on the one part; and Thomas Day the elder and Thomas Day the younger on the other part.
>
> It is hereby required that the said parties shall pull down so many of the walls of Barden Tower as the said Right Hon. Countesse hath lately appointed, and shall build both the walls of the said house and chapel as shall be thought fit, and shall repair all such windows, arches, doors and other places about the said house and chappel as shall be thought fit and necessary by the said Countesse, and shall raise a parpointe wall of a yard high for battlements round about ye said house.
>
> In consideration of the work above said the Countesse is to pay to the said parties the sum of £100.
>
> The said work is to begin in March and to be ended at Michaelmas, which shall be in the yeare 1657.

It is this work which now stands as the main part of the structure and the plan of the building is as Lady Anne knew it. The active life of the tower seems to have been in its earlier years, from about the 12th to the 16th century with a short revival in the mid-17th when it was certainly esteemed by Lady Anne as a summer residence for short periods.

(September 1963)

The Old House, Hetton   C.C. Cuthbert

NORTON TOWER:
A former jolly summer house

Norton Tower lies east of the Skipton to Grassington road and anyone passing along this road, within two miles of Skipton will notice the striking ruin standing on a prominent spur of hill below the great line of crags of Rilston Fell Edge, which culminate in the Stone Man, now a timber cross, above Norton Tower.

From all points of view the ruin has a romantic and tantalising appearance due to its shape and setting. Only the four corners remain, the centre parts of the four walls being pulled out when the tower was "slighted" nearly four hundred years ago. Below the ruins there is a steep wooded slope and on one side a deep rocky gill and noisy beck, Waterford Gill. Around and behind the Tower there is the rough moorland pasture of the Bark leading up on to the wild moorland mass of Barden Fell.

There is no precise date to be given for the erection of Norton Tower but in the records of the College of Arms it is stated "that Richard, last of the Nortons, builded a tower in the farthest part of his lordship of Rilston, near Crookrise. He used to lie in summer always at his house in Rillestone, which his grandfather or great-grandfather had by marriage of Radcliff's daughter and co-heir, which Radcliff's ancestor had formerly married Rillestone's daughter and heir."

Miles Radcliffe of Threshfield married Isabel de Rilston in 1434 and it was his grand-daughter Anne Radcliffe who married John Norton somewhere towards the end of the 15th century. Richard Norton was her son, born early in the 16th century.

The Old Hall, of which there are now no traces except the name and a few mounds in a field, was near Rilston church, and was their home, though it seems from the quotation given above that the family must have spent winters at the old family home of Norton Conyers, and only the summers at Rilston, where the tower was built for the recreation of the numerous family. With all this in mind one would venture a date soon after 1500 for its building.

The site of the tower is a small headland of rocky ground, jutting out from the general hillside and having a broad swampy hollow between it and the main breast of the fell, and with a deep stream course in a gill on one side, and on the other a very deep and swampy hollow running down from the swamps behind the grounds. The front of the site is a steep and wooded rocky slope, the whole position looking at first sight like a place chosen for defence and suited to that purpose.

The nearly level summit of this little hill is enclosed in a massive wall of which only a little remains here and there, and part of the wall is built on a broad bank with a deep ditch on the outer side. This bank and ditch continue all round the hill enclosing the steep slopes as well and, with a fence or palisade of timber on the bank, it would make a most efficient fence.

Within the flatter area on top of the hill there are several rectangular mounds, flat topped, built up and surrounded by broad, shallow ditches. Whitaker and others have suggested that these may have been butts for archery practice and this seems reasonable. There is also a large number (over 30) of small cairns of stones, which appear to have supported posts, and these, although no regular pattern can now be seen, may have been for jousting games or horsemanship, the area being extensive enough for such use.

The tower is a rectangular structure, 32 feet by 27 feet outside, with walls about four feet thick. There are the traces of a doorway on the south side and the beginnings of a stair in the south-east corner. The highest part is now 15 feet 9 inches, but may have been higher. The tower was "slighted"—that is, the mid part of each wall was pulled down to the ground level and the roof and all the floors destroyed—so that the building could never again be used.

The position is magnificent, with a splendid view across parts of Craven to Pendle Hill and over to the Malham Moors. Behind it the fell side rises to the great rock masses which edge the fell top. Across Waterford Gill, the new plantations remind one of the former Crookrise Forest which came to this gill as its boundary. Not far away the village of Rilston and its fields occupy the lower ground, and immediately below its hill, Scale House, then only a farm house, was the nearest dwelling. Flasby Fell and Skyracks stand just across the narrow valley of the Ellerbeck.

Richard Norton who built the tower was a man of some importance in the north of England. He was one of the family of Norton of Norton Conyers, had been a member of the Council of the North, and for some time Governor of Norham Castle, on Tweed. In 1567-8 he was High Sheriff of Yorkshire. He had a family which even in those days must be counted large, seven daughters and eleven sons, and no doubt the people of Rilston were well aware when the Norton family were in residence in the Hall, and no doubt it was some of these sons who delighted to use Norton Tower and made the many arrangements there for games and trials of skill.

In 1541 a serious quarrel had broken out between Norton and the Cliffords of Skipton Castle. Crookrise Forest had a common boundary in Waterford Gill with Rilston township, and a less well defined boundary on the high moor above, and the Cliffords were very fond of their hunting in Crookrise.

It becomes apparent that many of the deer strayed or habited on slopes of Rilston fell within the lordship of Rilston, and that the Cliffords did not scruple to conduct their hunts within that lordship boundary. Richard Norton questioned the Clifford right to "trespass" on his ground, and the matter was taken before the President and Council at York, and in the course of a few years many depositions were taken. These give an interesting picture of life at the middle of the century.

Several old men who at various times had been foresters for the Cliffords, in Crookrise or Old Park, said that they remembered in their youth, that Lady Clifford had often hunted and hounded deer in Rilston Lordship. Some of them however made it clear that they had hunted the deer "out of Rilston" into all parts of Skipton Forest, and one soon gets the picture that deer, claimed by the Cliffords to be strays, were in fact hunted or driven back out of Rilston ground into Skipton ground.

Richard Norton regarded these as his own deer, and Skipton officials regarded them as strays from Crookrise. There was even the accusation that

Norton had tempted and trapped these deer into his own land, by building "a wall on an high rigge, beside a quagmire, and at the end of the wall he hath rayled the ground, so that it is a destruction to my lord's deer, so many as come."

The outcome of this quarrel we do not know, but national events were developing that soon overshadowed any local quarrels. Norton was called to Norham and then to the duties of High Sheriff, and in the distance, the Earls of Northumberland and Westmorland were moving towards the Rising in the North, in their attempt to secure for Mary Queen of Scots, her liberty, the establishment of the succession in her favour, and the removal of evil counsellors. An appeal was made to the Catholic families of the north for support, and a ballad in the Percy collection of Ancient Ballads, says that the Earl of Northumberland sent a messenger to Richard Norton, asking his support, and that Richard took counsel of his sons. Of these Christopher advised that they join in the rebellion, but the eldest son Francis advised against any share in the venture.

Froude, the historian, says "The father, Richard Norton, was past middle life at the time of the Pilgrimage of Grace (1536). It may be assumed with confidence that he was one of the 30,000 enthusiasts who followed Robert Aske from Pomfret to Doncaster behind the banner of the Five Wounds of Christ ... one of his sons, Christopher, had been among the first to enrol himself as a knight of Mary Stuart ..." It is not clear how many Nortons joined in the rebellion, but Christopher and his uncle Thomas were executed at Tyburn, and Richard died an exile in Spanish Flanders.

With the failure of the rebellion all the estates of Richard Norton were confiscated for treason, and action was taken against the many ordinary folk who had supported the cause. Examples were made in all areas and then, after a number of executions, the rest were pardoned. The documents of the rebellion show that the Norton manors of Rilston, Linton, Threshfield, and part of Flasby and Hebden, were confiscated to the Crown. Orders were given that certain men on the list of rebels were to be dealt with.

"Men of Craven to be executed nyhe the townes where they dwelled ..." 23 Jan. 1569-70. "I will that you George Unes do Inventorye the goodes of these men within named to be executed, promysing the wyffes and children that I will be good to theym.

Lynton	Edward Wilkinson
	Nicholas Hewytt
Threshfield	Will. Whytacre als Stable
	Thomas Styrke
	Robert Araye
	Christopher Ratcliffe
Rylleston	Richard Kaley
	Richard Kitchin
	Wilfryde Smythe als Settle
	John Kygheley
Hanlith	Wm. Sergeantson
	(signed) George Bowes.

The rest of the rebels were pardoned on the 25th of April.

These events ended the Norton connection with Craven, and we can imagine something of the excitement and muttered threats that would follow the executions, which were carried out. It is certain that had the estates been given to some other person, straight after the executions, the new owners would have come across a lot of dour resistance and ill-will. However, the confiscated estates remained in the hands of the Crown until 1605 when they were granted to the Cliffords of Skipton, and soon after they received them, large portions of them were sold and became the freehold property of a new race of independent farmers and yeomen.

It is not surprising that these stirring events should have formed the basis of legend and story, but the stories, alas, are very inaccurate in detail and have given rise to much imaginary history. Of the older stories, the ballad in Percy's "Reliques of Ancient poetry" is probably near contemporary in date.

Probably the best known story is that preserved in Wordsworth's poem, *The White Doe of Rylstone*. Wordsworth was a visitor in Yorkshire in 1816, and spent some time with the Rev. W. Carr, Rector at Bolton Priory. Here Wordsworth was greatly impressed by the scenery and proposed to write a poem about it, and Carr suggested that an incident recited by Whitaker could well be a part of the poem.

Whitaker says, after discussing the grant of the Rilston estates to the Cliffords, in 1605, "At this time a white doe, say the aged people of the neighbourhood, continued to make a weekly pilgrimage from Rylstone over the fells to Bolton, and was constantly found in the Abbey Churchyard, during Divine Service, after which she returned home, as regularly as the rest of the congregation."

"At this time..." would be at least thirty years after the Nortons left Rilston, and Whitaker shows his evaluation of this as a legend by going on at length to quote similar white beasts which occur in legend in many places, both in this country and others, concluding "It is curious to observe in how many ways these picturesque animals have been employed by poetical and historical fiction."

Wordsworth produced his poem *The White Doe of Rylstone* and he and later writers credited the doe as the companion of Emily Norton, and it has generally been said that Francis Norton caught this white doe and gave it to his sister Emily. Legend also says that this Francis, who took no part in the rising and was indeed a Protestant, was murdered on Barden Fell by some of the resentful local people, and was buried at Bolton Priory. Emily, who had tamed the doe, took it with her as a companion on her regular journeys across the fell to her brother's grave, and after her death, the doe continued to make the journey on its own.

The first difficulty which one encounters in seeking the truth or otherwise of this legend is that in the Norton family, whose pedigree is known for several centuries, there was never a woman called Emily. It was a name never used in that family. All the sisters of Francis are known, but none have this name. Was Emily an invention of Wordsworth, or Carr, or who? If the doe was still travelling to Bolton at the return of the Cliffords, it had a very long life, though Whitaker's statement might be read as it has been wrongly quoted, "Not long after the dissolution..." which would bring it forward to about 1540. We are thus in trouble over the date implied in the legend, as well as the name Emily.

The death of Francis on Barden Fell rests only on legend and may be no more than romantic trimming to improve the story. The most curious extension of this legendary history is that made by Sutcliffe, when he allows a Rilston person, at the time of the rebellion, to bring Emily Norton to hide with the miller of Threshfield, and christens the little mill bridge over Threshfield Beck (here called Captain Beck) as Lile Emily's Bridge, to be used by her on her way to Linton church.

It would be curious for Emily, a Catholic in hiding, to be such a regular attender, as is implied, at the now reformed and Protestant church of Linton. I believe that we can discount all attempt to associate "Emily" with Threshfield, and recognise the bridge for what it is, a convenient bridge on the path between Threshfield and Linton church.

Another fragment of history which has been glamorised is the existence of Clifford's Tower, on the summit of Crookrise, and overlooking Norton Tower. This was a small tower of two rooms on the ground floor, probably not more than an outlook over the forest of Crookrise, commanding a fine view over most of the area. It was useful for the keeper and his staff to keep watch for poachers or other disturbance of the game.

Romance has to link this with Norton Tower and place Clifford and Norton face to face, arrayed for battle and foray across Waterford Gill, and to convert the Clifford-Norton dispute into a petty warfare. The leisurely progress of inquiry and reposition in the Council of the North over several years, and the responsible positions held by Norton, High Sheriff of Yorkshire, member of the Council, Governor of Norham Castle, discount the ideas of murder and bloody war which has been grafted on to this dispute and credited to Norton and Clifford towers.

Thus stands Norton Tower, a ruin of a former rather jolly summer house, which probably had no more than twenty or thirty years of active usage. When its builder, Richard, was exiled, the Tower was "slighted" in feudal tradition, and left lonely to give rise to romantic legend.

(November 1963)

MINING AND
THE DALES MINER

Aysgarth Falls   Dennis Mallet

SILVER MINES IN THE DALES

Among the many economic products of the Dales that have been noted by writers and historians, silver has perhaps received least attention, and yet notable quantities of silver have been produced, and at various times the silver has attracted widespread interest. The lead mines of the Dales are well known though little has yet been written of their fascinating and sometimes romantic story, but few of those who pride themselves most on their knowledge of the mines remember that silver has been one of their products.

The oldest documented mining in the Dales is that done under Roman supervision and control in Swaledale (the Hurst mines) and on Greenhow Hill. At these places lead was mined and smelted in the times of Hadrian, Trajan, and Domitian and certainly of most of the emperors between 60 A.D. and 160 A.D. The smelted lead was cast into pigs weighing about 175lbs each, and having on the underside an inscription cast in. Of these pigs, four are recorded from the dales, one with an inscription of Trajan, one of Hadrian, and two of Domitian. The latter are preserved, one at Ripley Castle and one at the British Museum. The inscription reads IMP. CAES, DOMITIANO AVG. COS. VII. and is thus dated as being made in the seventh year of the consulship of Domitian, the year A.D.81. These with most other Roman lead found in the country have been analysed, and prove to have been refined by the extraction of their content of silver.

There is abundant evidence that silver was equally attractive with the lead in the mining operations. All lead ores in this country carry a small proportion of silver which remains in the lead when smelted, but can be extracted in refining, and this extraction was carried out at all the Roman works in the dales area. The two pigs of lead from Greenhow were found alongside an old track leading down from the mines towards the ford over the Nidd at Hampsthwaite, to join the road from Addingham to Aldborough, lost or hidden en route, by the carrier, probably a native slave. This find near the mines, along with a Trajan pig near Nussey Knott, proves the extraction of the silver on the spot and not at some centralised refinery.

After the Roman working of the mines little more is heard of them, except occasional mention during the Saxon and Norman periods, until the monasteries secured extensive grants and opened up new sites as well as those worked by the Romans. There is every evidence that the monastic workers had forgotten the art of extracting the silver, and took the lead as it came from the first smelting for their uses. In the sixteenth and seventeenth centuries, the art of silver extraction was almost lost in this country, and we are told by more than one writer of the seventeenth century that much lead was exported from this country to Holland, there to have its silver extracted at great profit, the refined lead being resold here. The extraction of silver as an important article of commerce was developed about the years 1690 to 1700 and carried on in most parts of the country after that date.

About the year 1600 Sir Bevis Bulmer, later connected with lead, silver and gold mines in Scotland, brought workmen from the south and gentlemen from London, to work a silver mine in the Forest of Bowland, where he "got good stores of Silver Ore, that held about 65 pound per Tun." This mine was worked in a small way on several subsequent occasions, but was too remote and the veins too variable to allow of any very great or continuous development.

The mines lie in the valleys east of the Trough of Bowland, on the Brennand River and Whitendale River, near the junction of the two valleys. The oldest mine sites are on the shoulder between the two dales, where the suggestive name Good Greave (or mine) lies near two of the lodes. An old adit and many mine workings are seen in the ground immediately north of Brennand House, and also over the hill in the next valley, near Whitendale House. Webster, a Yorkshireman (author of two important books, one on minerals, and the other on witchcraft) writing in 1671, says that the London gentlemen returned to these mines in 1655, to reopen those that had proved so rich for Bulmer, but that "they being men neither of free Purses to follow such a Work, nor of skill or government fit to manage such an Enterprise", they failed to continue the mines.

With them was a chemist, Walter Basby, an old man who in the time of James I had been sent to Russia to establish the standard of the Russian coinage, and while there had travelled to the mines in Tartary, being captured by the Tartars and ransomed by the Emperor of Russia, and had had a long life of experience as an assayer of silver and lead. He being deserted by the London miners was given hospitality by Webster and while there they visited the mines and collected ores which on analysis yielded the same large quantity of silver. The remoteness of the district, however, and lack of any transport, combined with the imperfect knowledge of silver refining, made the venture uneconomic. The mines were again opened for a short time by the Clitheroe Mining Company in the eighteenth century, but their main produce was lead.

Another famous silver mine lies not far away, on the northern foothills of Pendle Hill, at Rimmington. This mine, called Skelhorn, was similar to those of Bowland, in the richness of the silver content of the ore in the upper part of the veins. In the time of Queen Elizabeth this mine was worked by Mr. Pudsey, of Bolton-juxta-Bolland, who extracted much silver from the ore. Webster and Basby found ore on the dumps carrying 26 pounds of silver in the ton, some years later. Pudsey was thought to have set up an illegal mint, and coined silver shillings, marked with an escallop as his mark, which were known in the district as Pudsey shillings. The escallop was the Tower Mint mark for the years 1584, 85, and 86, and supports the suggestion that Pudsey was counterfeiting national coinage. Webster heard from local people that he secured his pardon, but Pudsey's brother petitioned Charles I as follows:

> "To the Kings most excellent Majesty. The humble petition of Ambrose Pudsey., Esq., sheweth, that your petitioner, having suffered much by imprisonment, plunder, etc., for his bounden loyalty, and having many years concealed a Myne Royall in Craven, in Yorkshire, and prayeth a patent for digging and refining the same."

This is an interesting example of the law of mines royal, which gave the Crown right of possession and working of all mines that produce gold or silver sufficient to pay the cost of smelting and working the same. This act meant the forfeiture of a rich mine, and many mines in Craven and in Arkengarthdale and Swaledale were "concealed" and worked illegally. It is evident that

Skelhorn was so concealed, but under the penalties for coining the silver, the brother felt safety lay in petitioning for a royal Letters Patent to work the mine. A similar Letters Patent was secured in 1627 for the Bowland Mines.

> "1627, Nov. 30th. Grant to Sir Henry Mervyn, John Rudstone, & Thomas Webster, of the mines royal of the Forrest of Bowland and hundreds of Wyersdale, Staincliffe, and Ewecross, in cos. York and Lancaster, for 21 years, paying to the King after the first two years a tenth part of all the silver."

The mine at Rimmington was worked for a number of years, and as late as 1670 a few men were still getting some ore, but to avoid the claiming of the mine as a concealed royal mine, they were in the habit (as a contemporary account tells us) of mixing the silver rich ore with very poor ore from neighbouring veins and smelting the two together as an ordinary ore of low enough value not to be claimed. Skelhorn had many subsequent short periods of work, and in the last twenty years has from time to time produced a large quantity of barytes.

Following a repeal of the Acts affecting the forfeiture of a mine royal by William and Mary, and the change to the power of pre-emption on silver and gold ores at a fixed price, if the Crown desired to purchase them, the stimulus to the extraction of silver from lead was provided. With the introduction of the new types of furnace and technique, by the Quaker Lead Company, the extraction of silver from lead, became general after 1704. The large mining areas of Grassington, and Swaledale and Wensleydale expanded during the seventeenth century, and from their ordinary lead produced silver in quantities hardly dreamed of by the earlier silver miners. A few veins produced a silver rich ore, and some of this, from Bishopdale for instance, was sent to the Quaker Lead Company's smelt mill and refinery in Bollihope Burn, Weardale, for silver extraction, but most ores were refined at the local smelt mills. The figures of lead-silver production in Yorkshire are not all available, but so far as they go, they show that between 1850 and 1880 the yearly yield of silver was between six and seven thousand ounces from the mines that made returns. We can perhaps judge something by comparison with the Alston Moor and Teesdale area, where the output of lead was about the same, and where the silver extracted between 1815 and 1870 was over four and a half million ounces. The ores of that district were somewhat richer than those of Yorkshire, but it is probably an under-estimate to say that during the eighteenth and nineteenth centuries the dales produced two or three million ounces of silver from their lead mines.

A few mines were richer than normal, and had for some time the name of silver mines, some veins being known as Silver Rake (one of the best of the Kettlewell Mines) or some other equally suggestive name. Braithwaite Mine in Wensleydale and one of the Appletreewick mines for several years produced unusually large quantities of silver, but from the short duration of their ores, their output was in the long run less than poorer mines with a long life.

Until the middle of the eighteenth century the silver produced was sold to the Mint at the Tower of London, but after that time, was sold in the open market at Stockton, York or London, mainly to the silversmiths. All that remains today of this former silver industry, are a few derelict smelt mill sites with the ruins of refineries, and a few mine heaps and adits to mark the places where great riches were extracted.

(January 1940)

LEAD FROM THE GREY HILLS

Lead, iron and coal were all in use in Britain in Roman times and lead and iron were being made into many useful objects and tools at least a century before the Roman occupation. What is the evidence for the earliest periods of the mining industry in our Northern Dales? How much indisputable evidence is there, and how much is inference or merely tradition?

If we look to the pre-Roman times, we must admit that while we know a very large number and variety of objects made of lead and iron, found in caves and hut-circles of Iron Age occupation, we know nothing of their source. In Ireland the Bronze Age people worked the gold of the Wicklow Hills and tin was worked from the stream gravels of Cornwall in the late Bronze Age and Iron Age, so there was certainly some knowledge of mining among the pre-Roman people.

Roman writers tell us that among other things Britain was known and desired for its metals, and soon after the Roman conquest lead mines were actually at work in the south west and producing lead on a large scale. Native labour was used in many mines, and in some of them political and military prisoners were made to labour as convicts. There is indirect and circumstantial evidence enough to say that in some parts of the country mines had been worked in a primitive sort of way before ever the Romans set foot in the country, and that in some cases the first task of the Romans was to re-organise the native miners and bring them under Roman supervision.

In the Northern Dales, apart from numerous objects of metal, including a gold coinage, the first indisputable evidence of mining is Roman. In the case of lead, the best evidence is that of a number of pigs of cast lead (oblong ingots of about a hundredweight and a half) which have an inscription cast on to them by which their date and place of origin can generally be determined. Four such pigs came from the Yorkshire Dales, several from the Derbyshire Dales and four from the Humber. Many fanciful and grossly inaccurate references have been made to them, so it might be as well to indicate just what they are and what they carry in the way of inscriptions.

In 1735 a horseman riding down Hayshaw Bank, near Dacre, in Nidderdale, discovered through the stumbling of his horse two pigs of lead, hidden in a hole on the track side. The pigs are identical except for a pound difference in weight; 23¾" long, 5¾" wide, and tapering a little to the bottom. Their weights are 155 and 156 lbs.

On the bottom surface there is a raised inscription which has been made by cutting the letters into the bottom of the mould in which they were cast. The inscription is:

IMP. CAES. DOMITIANO. AVG. COS. VII.

and, like all Roman inscriptions, is considerably contracted. Expanded, it would read "Imperator Caesar Domitiano Augustus. Consul VII" and indicates that it was cast in the year of the seventh consulship of Domitian, that is the year 81 A.D.

On one side of the pig there is a slighter inscription, the single word BRIG, indicating that the lead came from the territory of the Brigantes, the native tribe of the mid Pennines. Another pig of lead with a TRAJAN inscription was found on Nussey Knott, between Greenhow Hill and Hebden, sometime before 1885, and that pig must belong to the period round about 98 A.D. These three would be cast from lead got on Greenhow and Nussey Knott.

The fourth Roman pig of lead from the dales is the one from the Hurst Mine, near Marrick, in Swaledale, now lost, but recorded soon after its discovery as having an inscription with the name of the emperor Hadrian, and so belonging to the years between 117 A.D. and 138 A.D.

At Brough-on-Humber three pigs of lead have been found and a fourth similar one at South Cave, all with the inscription

C. IVL. PROTI. BRIT. LVT. EX. ARG.

This can be expanded and translated as "the property of Caius Julius Protus; British lead from Lutudarum, from the silver works".

Another pig was also found at Brough-on-Humber with an inscription of a very unusual type:

SOC. LVT. BRIT. EX. ARG.

– "property of the company of British mines of Lutudarum, from the silver mines." As Brigantia was part of the Pennines which includes all Craven and further north, so Lutudarum was Derbyshire, and we can see that the lead was sent from Derbyshire to the Humber for export to Italy or France. The Yorkshire lead was being carried along a track from Greenhow to Boroughbridge, where it could be carried down the river to the same port, while the Swaledale pig could go by the Swale to the Humber, or to the Tees at Yarm.

The various inscriptions tell us much about the organisation of the mines. In Yorkshire the mines were imperial property, worked by the forced labour of native prisoners and managed by Roman officers, and all their produce was marked with the imperial stamp. In Derbyshire, where the mines may be of a slightly different date, the mines were entirely the property of merchant-freemen and, in one case, of a society of free British merchants. Some of the Derbyshire lead was carried to the Humber for export, but some went by other routes, by Nottingham and to the south.

All our records of Roman mining finish by the decade 150 A.D. to 160 A.D. and after that, if the mines continued, they were probably worked by free natives who have left us no recognisable evidence of their work. We have no other direct evidence than that set out above. The pig of lead reported from Castlesteads, nr. Pateley, by Mr. Speight, is of late medieval or even later date. The two Hayshaw Bank pigs can be seen – one in the British Museum, and one in Ripley Castle.

All other evidence of Roman mining in Yorkshire is still open to doubt. It cannot rank higher than a likely probabilty or is, unfortunately, now incapable of verification. It has been said that on Greenhow Hill there are two old levels, the Jackass and Sam Oon levels, which are Roman, and it is reported that Roman pottery was found in one of them.

This pottery was given to Mr. Crowther, of Grassington, by a workman who is un-named, and as it was never labelled it cannot now be identified in his collections. The section and method of working the levels resemble Roman work. But they are not unlike much work of late medieval date, which they might possibly be. In Grass Wood, Grassington, a Roman coin and some pottery were reported as found in an old mine working. Again, they were neither labelled nor critically examined at the time, and though they might possibly be correct, we cannot assert it as positive evidence. Further, the workings where they were found are very near to the hut circles which were excavated and which yielded much Roman pottery and some coins.

Far from being an argument for the truly Roman date of the workings, this merely adds the likelihood that the stuff was stray from these excavations, and the workings themselves are of sixteenth or seventeenth century date, for which date we have some records. Similar difficulties to all these occur with the story of the actual mine workings at Hurst Mine, Swaledale. The pig of lead was found near them, but the mine levels that have been described could well be much later in date.

For the mining and smelting of iron there is very scant evidence, although the industry must have been pretty widespread in the Huddersfield to Bradford area. At Low Moor and in Bierley district slag heaps have been found with Roman coins in the slag and closely associated, and these are very definite and satisfactory evidence. Of the actual mining site we know very little, or possibly nothing. There are many areas which by the argument of analogy and likelihood will stand high in any list of probabilities but which cannot be placed as certainties.

In several parts of Yorkshire and the northern dales the Romans established potteries and tile-yards, and in many areas worked the clays needed for these products. Near Huddersfield, about two miles north-west of the town, Roman workings were discovered in Grimescar Wood, from which the Hard Bed Band fire-clay had been mined. This clay was made into tiles, on the spot, and the tiles marked with a stamp of the cohort in charge of the work. Several of these stamped tiles are to be seen in the Tolson Museum, Huddersfield.

In East Yorkshire, the Cram Beck clay was used for an extensive Roman pottery, and potteries with kilns are found there and at Throlam Farm, near Holme-on-Spalding Moor.

We can state in summary that beyond the pigs of lead, with dateable and localised inscriptions, from Greenhow and Swaledale, we have little positive evidence in Yorkshire which would encourage one to be dogmatic and say, "Here the Romans worked mines." At the same time there is indirect evidence that the working of lead, iron and clays was quite an important feature of the Roman occupation and was probably continued by the natives after their retreat.

After the withdrawal of the Romans there was a little mining in the pre-Conquest years, and mines in Derbyshire are mentioned in the Domesday Survey. Our records further north, however, are very scanty until the monastic period, the fourteenth to sixteenth centuries.

This was the next great chapter in the story followed, after a break of about a century, by the widespread activity of the "free-miners", leading before 1800 to the modern and latest section of the story. There is not much detail of the actual work and methods of the earlier miners but many MSS have survived which give an intimate picture of day to day activities of the free-miners, with crude account books that show the level of the wages and prices and the forms of contract under which the miners worked. To describe and discuss this evidence would need a large volume, but a little of the story can be illustrated by dipping into one small account book and taking from it sufficient items to give a connected picture.

The MS we will use is a little homemade book of yellowish paper. Its pages are 6½" by 8", made by folding eight foolscap sheets in half and then sewing them together into a cover of very coarse brown paper. The cover has on it:

> "Blackhill Book 1771
> Robt. Stockdale Ripon
> End 1775 Mine"

The first accounts do not quite fill the first eight pages, and all relate to the Black Hill mine, on the east side of the upper part of Trollers Gill, Appletreewick. The rest of the book is about a mine on Ripon Vein, Grassington Moor, and the workings include a few references to Grimes Grove and Sword and Pistol, two smaller veins near the Ripon. The book was kept by the foreman at Black Hill and taken with him to the Ripon Vein when he changed his job in 1775.

His writing is fairly good for the period, but his spelling, especially of personal names, is mainly guesswork, based on sound only, Nid (Ned), Mikil (Michael), Anty (Anthony), Gorg (George) being only a few of his attempts. For Black Hill the accounts are mainly notes of "bargains" but for the Ripon Vein there are more notes of purchase of materials for the mine and more information about the prices paid for ore and lead.

The Black Hill mine had been working for some time, but when the account opens extensions were being made, and the first entry, in July 1771, is:

> Jon Gyte 19 shifts at Stuffey Shaft at 16d. pr. [shift].
> Jon Marshall 15 shifts at Do. at 16d. pr.

The shifts were often of twelve hours, so that the wage was about three half-pence an hour. The shaft was being sunk and was already well down as the next entry, 15th July, is a bargain:

> "Then let John hoult & Son to Drive north west in the forfield 5 Fathm at 12s. 6d. pr. Fathm and for all the ore is got in the above Drift is to have £7 pr. tun for every Clear tun of Lead, they pay all expenses as usual."

At this time the shaft was some five fathoms deep (thirty feet) and Hoult and his son started the level which was to be driven along the vein at this depth. The payment is very typical of most of the mine bargains – a fixed price for the length, 12s. 6d. a fathom of six feet, and then £7 a ton extra for all the lead which was smelted from the ore they produced during the driving of the level.

The "bargain" was already a speculative balance between these two factors. If rock was hard and very little ore was expected, then a high price, 16s. or 17s. a fathom, was paid; if ore was thought likely to be abundant, then a low price would be offered for the driving and most of the wages could be made from the lead.

One bargain states "... six tun of Clear lead at £8 a tun or if it prove a hard bargain will pay £8.8 pr. tun." Another level was planned eight fathoms deeper than the first, to be reached by a small shaft or sump, sunk from the first level.

> "The let John Marshall John Gyte a Sump-head to cut 1 Fathm and 7 Fathm in a Sump to sink and the Drive to the Side Stone at £1.5. pr. Fathm and at Sump foot to Drive 10 Fathm as near to the Side Stone as is possible to make a sufficient Drift at 10s. pr. Fathm and is to have 8 Clear tun of Lead to get at £7 pr. tun and is to get the ore in the forefield or on the rise side is to Pay all expenses as usual and make sufficient work in drifts and all works."

A mineral vein usually occupies a small fault and the sides of the vein are clearly marked "walls" or, as he calls them, side stone. As a vein is not quite vertical, a shaft sunk from a point in the vein, vertically downwards, will gradually be further away from it as it gets deeper, so that at the foot of the shaft it is always necessary to make a short cross cut to reach the side stone. As that is through barren rock, the rate of pay is higher than where ore might be expected.

After reaching the side stone, a level can be driven along the vein and the ore is got at the forfield – that is, at the end of the level as it drives forward, or from the rise that is above the level. The miners paid all the costs of gunpowder, tools and candles, and many other sundries, but the mine owner provided all timber and certain other stores.

When the shaft was completed and the mine ready to work new bargains were made.

> "The let John Summersgill Gorge Peart and Jaack Leech two meers of ground
> 30 yards in Length to one meer of ground . . . etc."

From a very early date the lead veins were measured in meers of length, while all other work in the mine was measured in fathoms. We find meers and moor-meers mentioned in some of the Bolton Priory leases of the Appletreewick mines. The meer was probably of Anglo-Saxon origin and its length had been decided in a peculiar way. The miner was to have "his hact throw two wayes after the rake; and note that he that throw hact must stand in his pit or groove to the girdle or wast." This total throw of the hammer, two ways along the vein, made the length of the meer around thirty yards.

When the meers were claimed by a miner the Barmaster of the Mineral Court, held for all the district, had to give his sanction and record the grant, then measure off the meers along the ground. In most cases the miner made a mark or put up a rough stone to mark the boundaries of his meer. The "meer stone" usually had on it the initials of the miner or the partnership, and if the meer was at a place where the vein was first opened out, the stone would have F, or FOUNDER in addition.

There are meer stones in abundance on Grassington Moor, though they are now difficult to find after nearly two hundred years' neglect. Some of them have the initials J.S. and J.L. on them and might be marking the veins leased to Summersgill and Leech. In this present grant it is noted that the miners pay the usual expenses but that the masters provide the Rools and Ropes – the Jack roller for winding the ore up the shaft.

There are many more bargains recorded, as they were made or remade at least every three months or more, usually every month. We can look now at a few prices of materials. First, there are large quantities of small props and boards needed for lining the shaft and drifts in bad ground; such as "by 600 Stop rods at 4d. pr. 100," "two Dozen of ash wood at 2s. 3d. pr. Doz." These items are very frequent, and with them are items from the woodmen – pick shafts at 2d. each, which would be re-sold to the miners. The "wood" and "boards" are the sawn timber for framing in the shafts and drifts, and the "stop rods" are smaller stuff for packing behind the framing.

The greatest enemies of the miner were water and bad air and to deal with these we have accounts for "3 Fathom of Pumps at 6s. pr. Fathm" and "3 Fathm wind trunks at 2s. 3d. pr. Fathm." The pumps were made from tree trunks, bored and shaped to fit together with a spiggot joint. They were massive and, after being made in the woods, were probably carried on pony back to the mines. Our account is "Paid mickel Lambert for i Tun Pumps at 6s. pr. Tun carried by my man."

Wind trunks were square pipes made of light wood and about eight or nine inches square. These were carried down the shaft and through the drifts, on brackets, and air was blown down them, either by a hand worked fan or bellows or by a large wooden cowl on top of the trunks, sometimes called the "horsehead".

Access to the mine was generally made by "stemples" in the shaft and not by ladders. The stemples are wood props set across the corner of the shaft, usually at intervals of about a yard, and the miner simply climbed up and down them with the occasional addition of a toe hold in the side of the shaft. Workings followed the vein, twisting and climbing about, and "winzes" from one level to another were merely narrow, twisting creep ways, sufficiently slanted to be climbed by an active person brought up to use them.

During all the years covered by the accounts, the work of the mines, both at Black Hill and Ripon End, was let out by bargains to partnerships of two, three, or four miners. The ore which they got was dressed near the mine, either by themselves or by boys and sometimes by women whom they employed for the job. The dressed ore, ready for smelting, is always to be delivered at the Mill bank: that is, at the smelt mill yard.

The smelter kept enough finished lead to pay for their labour, fuel, etc., and also one fifth was kept back by the steward of the manor as the royalty. What was left was then the clear produce of the miners' work. The mine manager or agent now paid the miner his agreed price, £7 or £8 a ton for his lead, then sold it to the lead merchants for what he could get. In most cases in the accounts we are dealing with the selling price was £12 15s. a ton.

The bargain system meant that the free miners could change their work every few months if conditions did not please them. They could make their own bid for the kind of work they liked or for the places where they thought a large surplus of ore might be got.

In this way they had considerable independence and the chance to make an occasional lucky strike or a particularly good bargain. In the worst of cases they would have a basic rate for the cutting they did, so were never actually penniless so long as they were prepared to take a bargain. This bargain work of free miners seems to have been the main type of mining in the dales lead areas from about 1600 to the early part of the nineteenth century, when larger companies sprang up, and much more work was done as hired labour for a fixed wage.

In the free miner period there was an abundance of small shafts scattered from end to end of the larger veins and a constant exploration in search of new ground and better bargains. This was the period when practically all the field was opened up, leaving very little new ground for the later companies, who mainly developed deeper workings.

(January 1951)

WATER WHEELS
AT THE MINES

A great event in mining history was the publication in 1556 of Agricola's *De Re Metallica*, a big book which dealt with every aspect of mining from prospecting and surveying, through the working of mines and ore dressing, to the smelting and refining of ores and metals. The volume was illustrated with a large number of excellent woodcuts of mines and of every description of mine processes and equipment. Many of the plates show water wheels employed in lifting from the mine, in working pumps, in ore dressing and in driving the furnace bellows. The book reflects the general mining practice of Europe and was widely known and used by miners in many countries.

In 1565 German miners were opening the copper mines around Keswick and they introduced to them many of the Continental methods of working, and in particular made good use of water wheels which they used for driving stamps to crush the ore (the accounts include such items as "Stamp in Newlands, Wolff Prugger, carpenter, 15 days at 8d, cutting axle for the water wheel, 10/-") as well as for the bellows at the smelt mills. Their work was well known and they helped to spread the knowledge of the new methods described by Agricola.

Lead mining was an ancient occupation in the Dales area, having a history starting in pre-Roman times, but it is not until the seventeenth century that it began to develop on a large scale when attempts were made to sink mines to new depths which demanded better means of drainage and haulage. For much of that century the shafts were wound by means of the horse gin, and horses were also used to work the necessary pumps.

While horses could be yoked to perform these tasks it was difficult to apply their strength to work bellows. It was far easier to use the water wheel for bellows, as the rotating shaft with nogs (projecting lugs) could be arranged so that the nogs in turn could force down the top boards of one or two bellows. There were, of course, counterbalance weights to pull the boards up again and inflate the bellows for the next stroke. At an early date two bellows side by side were arranged to blow alternately, one blowing, one filling, so keeping a steady blast.

Bellows were used in the iron industry in the forges and furnaces, and water wheels also operated the larger trip hammers. Before 1700 the iron industry between Kirkstall and Sheffield was equipped with a large number of such wheels and there was one at the iron mill at Fewston. During the eighteenth century the horse gin was still the common method of drawing ore up the mine shaft, and nearly all the water wheels used in connection with the mines were the small ones at the smelt mills.

Among early mills were those at Grassington – the Low Mill opposite Linton Church on the river bank but using water from Brow Well, was working before 1650 and continued until about 1770 when it was replaced by the Cupola on Grassington Moor, which had been built about twenty years earlier. There was also the Old Mill on Grassington Moor, just to the west of the Cupola, but little is known of the history of this mill and little remains but traces of the foundations and a good deal of slag. The High Mill at Buckden (Birks Mill south of the river and half a mile up Water Gill) was working in 1704 and so was the Low Mill at Starbotton. Kilnsey and Kettlewell mills were brought into operation during the century, and towards the end of the century the Smelt Mill on Malham Moor. All these had small water wheels to drive the bellows. In the opening years of the nineteenth century more mills were blown in, one at Cononley and some on Greenhow.

The greatly increased production of lead in the second half of the eighteenth century stimulated the search for better and more economical methods of dressing the ore prior to smelting. Stamps were introduced to this area for ore crushing and consisted of a battery of vertical rods shod with heavy cast iron feet, the rods being lifted by nogs on a water wheel shaft and then let drop on the ore placed under them. After 1804 roller crushing mills were used, and again they were driven directly by a water wheel.

One old method of ore dressing included shaking the crushed ore on a riddle suspended in a tub of water and from this many inventions stemmed for a variety of power-driven machines, sieves, jiggers, hotching tubs and so on, again driven directly from a water wheel and performing the processes with greater speed and efficiency.

Pumping to keep the mine workings dry was an increasing burden, and to work pumps a straight up and down motion was necessary. This could be got from a water wheel when a crank moved a connecting rod back and forward and so operated a bell-crank lever (an L-shaped lever). This motion could be transmitted to a distance from a convenient wheel through rods hung from a line of supports. In fact the wheel only had to lift the pump rods, their own weight on the downstroke being usually quite enough to work a force pump.

All these new demands for power set the engineers seeking out available water, a task by no means as simple as that of the spinners, who could place their mill on a convenient large stream. Many, in fact most, mines were on the high fells, with little or no surface water, and high above the stream valleys. Great effort was expended in making dams wherever there was a usable trickle of water to be collected.

Over the moors in the mining areas there are miles of small water courses, now almost silted up and overgrown, leading from the higher slopes to a variety of small pools, often shallow and only impounded by a turf dam, now more often than not collapsed and the pool represented by a swampy area of peaty mud.

A few of the ponds are of large size, such as Priest Tarn, on the highest part of Grassington Moor towards Meugher. Here a broad natural hollow between two parts of the moor was spanned at each end by a big turf and timber dam and a complex of small drains and cuts was made to collect as much as possible of the heavy rainfall of the area. This "tarn" became a breeding place for gulls, and early in this century one dam was broken and the tarn was drained. Other large dams are the three on Blea Beck connected with the Grassington mines, now almost drained, and the Mossy Mire Dam built for the Hebden mines and still in good condition.

The increased efficiency of the improved water wheels designed by Smeaton made it possible to pump and haul from greater depths and this resulted in an increase in the output of ore, thus putting considerable strain on the capacity of the ore dressing floors. The real shortage of water above ground led to the practice of using the same stream of water over and over again, so that a supply would be taken over several wheels in turn and also pass through several dressing floors. Before the water finished its work it must have become as thick as mud. The introduction of mechanical dressing called for wheel power, and in the early years of the nineteenth century there was something like a power crisis, the solution of which shows remarkable mechanical ingenuity.

The limiting size of a water wheel was determined by the quantity of water available and the speed at which the wheel was required to run. The quantity of water depended upon collecting numerous small sources into a dam, and even when this was accomplished there remained a fine balance of possibilities. If the water were wanted for a dressing floor wheel or a mill, was it better to have a large dam, rest a long time until it was filled, and then run a large wheel and work up the accumulated ore in a great rush of heavy work? Or was it better to have a small wheel with a smaller dam, but run more or less continuously at a much less volume of work?

These were very urgent questions and were answered in different ways on different mines. It is good fun to trace out water courses and the pool they fed, then take the outflow from the pool to the wheel pit, judge the size of the floors or mill it serves, and try to answer the questions for that site. In the case of a corn or cotton mill wheel, the location is near a river or large stream, and water trouble is more likely to be caused by flood than by drought; the wheel and mill are of interest, but they present very few problems. In contrast with this almost every wheel or group of wheels on a dressing floor or for a mine pump, sets a unique problem which only a close study of the rainfall and topography and the analysis of the remains of water courses, can solve.

A major requirement for wheels operating pumps was that they should have continuous working or the underground workings would flood. A frequent arrangement was for the wheel to run normally off a stream with good capacity, the water brought by a water course which sometimes was very long, and then have cut-off arrangements and courses so that when there was more water in the stream than the wheel required, the surplus was run off into a storage pond from which it could be drawn when the stream was inadequate. Such an arrangement involved a complex of water courses, sluices and alternative courses, and an amount of levelling that called for great ingenuity and considerable skill in hydraulic engineering. To get the greatest advantage for these much bigger wheels, they were placed as low down a stream course as possible, and the power from them carried to the mines by suspended rods or wire ropes. If there was a very good supply of water available, one big wheel (50 feet or more in diameter) might serve several mines with more than one set of rods and several ropes.

In Hebden Gill and at the mouth of Bolton Gill there is a fairly simple example of this. A wheel pit can still be seen with a long watercourse starting from the stream just below a dam (now broken) high up on Bolton Gill. This watercourse takes in from the stream at about 1,130 feet O.D. and runs a mile round the flank of Bolton Haw to a reservoir, the Mossy Mire Dam, at 1,020 feet O.D., then back round the hill in a culvert to a point above the water wheel which is at about 960 feet O.D. There is a connection between the two sections of the culvert so that water can travel directly from the stream to the wheel, leaving the dam to be filled when there is any excess of water or to be drawn upon when there is a drought.

From the wheel one set of rods went along the side of Hebden Gill about 300 yards to the coal shaft, to work a set of pumps there, and another went in the opposite direction for a short distance. There it connected with a double bell-crank lever in a pit on the shoulder of the hill, which turned the rods through a right angle to go up Bolton Gill to the shaft top at Bolton Gill Mine, at 1,100 feet O.D. There was also a winding rope from the water wheel, round a horizontal turn wheel and so up to the shaft. Similar as well as more complicated arrangements are found in many parts of the Pennines.

Where a good water supply was possible it was often an economy to concentrate as many processes as possible at that point. An example from Grassington will suffice to illustrate this point, and will also emphasise the great skill in levelling and setting out water-courses that was exercised by the miners a hundred and fifty years ago. There is a good stream high up Grassington Moor, which was tapped for the mine dressing floors, and which was also run into the three Blea Beck storage dams when water was plentiful. There was a system of draw offs which made any of the dams available at any time, by different routes.

At the old High Grinding Mill there was a wheel which became the centre of activity about the beginning of the nineteenth century. Near it was built the timber yard with a small saw mill with a ten-foot wheel. Then there were added the High Winding House with a 35 foot wheel and a winding rope going some distance over the moor to wind the Moss Mine. Another and much larger wheel was put in at a place called the Brake House, then the watercourses were so arranged that all these wheels could take water from the original stream water course, or from the upper Blea Beck Dams.

The Brake House wheel which wound four mines and must be kept going in all seasons, could draw off the Blea Beck Dams at any point and from the stream. There was a complex of short cross water courses so arranged that any wheel could be isolated and any combinations of wheels could be run, with the same water going over them all in succession.

If we take together the wheels for the smelt mills, those for grinding, pumping and for winding, they mount up to a large number, at least forty in Upper Wharfedale and Greenhow Hill.

(May 1961)

LIFE IN THE LEAD MINES

There is now available, in increasing number, books on lead mining in this country, and journals like those of the Peak District Mines Historical Society and the Northern Cavern and Mines Research Society are regularly publishing papers on mines and mining history. However an examination of this literature soon reveals that the bulk of it is concerned either with the history of mining in general, processes, the technology of mining, tools and apparatus or with the economic history of mining ventures. It is rare to find any direct reference to the conditions in which men worked or to the effect of their work on their health and their life. It is very true that in the documentary sources for mining history earlier than the Royal Commissions of the nineteenth century, the direct evidence for the conditions of work is sparse and scattered.

An increasing knowledge of the physical character and dimensions of the miners' work place belonging to more than one period is being revealed by the many groups who are exploring old mines. These results have to be used with caution as the places explored have either been worked or reworked in the latest periods of mining, or have suffered centuries of neglect and are in far worse condition than when they were worked. There is a need for serious research into the human aspects of every part of the lead miners' work comparable with that which some historians have directed to life in the coal mines.

If we are to attempt what can only be a very sketchy account of the miners' working conditions, not more in fact than a suggestion in general terms of what could be the subject of organised and intensive research, we shall need a framework in which to view our evidence. Lead mining needs to be looked at as an occupation with at least three strongly contrasted sections which have very little in common except the purpose of producing lead as an eventual marketable product.

The miner is the "getter" – he works mainly underground boring his way through rock in tortuous and confined ways to break out the ore and get it to the surface. The "dresser" takes the rough product of the mine, ore, rock and spar mixed, crushes it, and by various manipulations separates the lead ore from the waste and prepares if for the smelter. This work except in the nineteenth century was done in the open air, the dressers being subject to exposure to every kind of weather. The smelter worked under cover in the smelt mill but was continuously exposed to the heat and glare of the furnaces and to air fouled by fumes. One could hardly imagine three such different working environments.

In addition to these three main groups there were ancillary workers who however are not peculiar to mining – the large number of carriers, blacksmiths necessary for the making and maintenance of tools, and clerks to keep count of production, wages and costs, etc. We shall not be concerned in this article with more than the three primary groups, ore getters, dressers and smelters, though within the group of getters one must for convenience include a few specialist jobs – level arching, timber setting, shaft sinking and the like.

Because lead ore occurs in veins which are thin and near vertical, the workings usually follow the vein to a depth which may amount to many hundreds of feet (always in the mines measured in fathoms of two yards). The ore in a vein may be a rib not more than an inch or two thick or may be scattered in a mass of spar or rock, and will be only a small part of the material which the miner has cut out to make working room for himself. Much of his work is driving through solid rock and he is always constrained to cut only the minimum room which will allow him to get the ore. This applies in shafts and tunnels as well as in the actual working places in the vein. He must work nearly always in closely confined spaces, he moves about in the mine through tunnels and passages which just allow his passage and as the mine develops he will have to climb from level to level by narrow shafts, "rises" and "winzes" or even by sloping and tortuous creep ways only sufficiently out of the vertical to make it possible for him to climb them without a ladder. The physical effort demanded, only to move about the mine, can be excessive. For anyone with the slightest trace of claustrophobia even to enter the mine would be impossible.

In the early days of mining, a vein being discovered at the surface was worked by open cast, it being dug from a long trench whose depth could not be very great for fear of a collapse of the sides. In this the work was not greatly different from that of the navvy except for the greater prevalence of hard rock. The work was however in the open air with full exposure to the weather. Soon the vein would have to be followed underground either by shafts or by levels and these soon reached the "water table", the permanent level of ground water saturation. Here the miner met with one of his major enemies. Every hole cut into the water table, every shaft, level or working place dripped water, and if not drained by an *adit* (a tunnel driven specifically to drain a mine and made from the lowest available point of a nearby valley), or by pumps of some sort, the mine soon filled and was completely drowned out.

However good the drainage might be the working places and levels of the mine were always wet. The clothes the miner could wear were always wet and stiff with rock dust and clay. In the late eighteenth century some companies like the London (Quaker) Lead Company introduced the mine *shop*, a building near the mines where a semi-retired miner kept a constant fire and where men coming out of the mine could change and leave their wet clothes to be partially dried overnight. Even with this provision the miner spent the bulk of his working hours in wet conditions often walking long distances underground to his working area along adits ankle deep in running water. The wet was increased below adit level and only constant pumping made work possible in these lower levels. If there were no shop then the miner had to go home in his wet working clothes and had little facility for drying them.

On some mines a few men were able to lodge not far away from their work. In 1715 for instance there were houses at a few mines in Swaledale. Level House at Old Gang had in addition to the person who lived there permanently, and his furniture, three spare bedsteads and a chaff bed; Old Level House had three beds of "joined boards". Ann Stapper (a washer) had in her house two bedsteads and Simon Bayles also had two. These bedsteads were large wooden frames with an under-mattress of rope mesh netting and a straw or chaff mattress on that, and in most cases they accommodated three or four men. Philip Lord Wharton in the late seventeenth century provided near Healaugh, for the Old Gang miners, Gang Hall which served as a hostel with a resident warden-smallholder, and accommodated a few of his miners. At best however such lodgings only catered for a small proportion of the single men.

Before his work began the miner often had a walk of a few miles over wild moorland and fells fully exposed to storm, wind and rain and could, if there were no shop, be already soaked through before he entered the mine. The journey to and from his working place underground might be hundreds of yards along narrow, wet levels, or involve hundreds of feet of an exhausting climb on ladders in the shaft. In some mines there were climbing shafts, rectangular and narrow enough to stride across. Small pigeon holes were provided in the masonry lining on opposite sides by which the miner could climb straddled across the depth beneath him. Some small shafts had "stemples" which were short lengths of timber set across the corners of the shaft and used as a ladder, often straddling across from one set to the other.

In deep mines the climbing could be so exhausting as to be a major hazard to health. It was felt to be a great concession when about the end of the eighteenth century with wider shafts, ladders ceased to be vertical and continuous on one shaft wall, and were set in lengths between stagings. The lengths were about twenty or thirty feet and the staging allowed the foot to be brought out four or five feet from the wall. It thus gave a slight inclination to the ladder, making the climb very much easier, and each staging allowed a few minutes' pause to get breath before the next length.

Arriving at the working face or *forefield*, the main work was breaking out the rock by pick, hammer and wedge. Fine cracks in the rock were opened out with a sharp pointed pick and an iron wedge with steeled point driven in with a sledge hammer to break off a pitifully small piece of rock. In driving a level an advance in very hard rock might only be a few inches in a day, with two men at work. A boy often accompanied his father into the mine from the age of nine or ten, and spent much of his time dragging the material, *bouse*, to the foot of the shaft. This was done either on a low sledge or in a sack, many of the working levels being too narrow for a barrow way.

In the eighteenth century gunpowder began to be used. Deep holes were drilled in the rock face by power of a hand drill and a very heavy sledge hammer, one man holding the drill and one striking, and the men alternating jobs in spells. Gunpowder was placed and stemmed in the hole and if properly placed broke off much larger rock than could be got by wedges. The powder made smoke and fumes and used up air so that the increased rate of working was got at the expense of a fouler air for the miner to breathe and work in. An absolute essential was always ventilation, a supply of air which the miner could breathe. If the air was so deficient that a candle would scarcely burn, a man would give up working, but the necessity of earning drove countless men to work as near as possible to this limit. Add to the lack of fresh air the wetness, the fumes, the dust and the miserable light of one or perhaps two tallow dips, and you begin to visualise something of the conditions in which the excessively heavy work of the miner was done.

Ventilation was always a problem in the long dead-end levels and working places. In Lownathwaite mines in Swaledale in 1685 the problem was very pressing and a report says "they found it was darker of wind (referring to the failure of a candle to burn well) that he took a fan down into the ground to help wind which would not do but was forced to carry down a pair of bellows which did much to help." If it was possible to have two shafts at a good distance from one another connected, or a shaft and a level, a natural draught would be created at least through a part of the mine but this would hardly extend into the working places. One of the greatest benefits of compressed air drills in the nineteenth century was that they constantly poured fresh air from their exhaust into the working places and carried away fumes and bad air.

The cumulative effect of all these bad conditions was evidenced in the prevalence of asthmas and other pulmonary diseases. Even in the nineteenth century in spite of all the advances in methods, the Kinnaird Commission on Health and working conditions found for the years 1860 to 1862 that of men between the ages of 45 and 55 more than twice as many died among miners (33 per thousand) as men in other occupations. Of these there were over four times as many deaths from lung diseases as among other workers. The London Lead Company followed by others had tried to reduce this danger by providing allotments and small holdings and encouraging their miners to spend regular days in work on them in the open air.

When the mixed ore and rock was got to the surface it had to be prepared for the smelter by getting rid of rock and spar, leaving a high *concentrate* of ore. The dressing was almost entirely the job of women and girls and boys, and was done in the open air, very seldom with any protection from the weather. The processes involved from the beginning of the seventeenth century were first to take the lumps of rock and spar and break off from them any visible bits of ore. This was *spalling*, done with a short-hafted heavy hammer and it meant continuous heavy work and handling large lumps of rock. It was usually the work of younger and stronger women and it was generally the tradition that the job was kept until marriage. The residual rock with ore in it was crushed with a *bucker*, a heavy flat-faced hammer, by boys standing at a *knockstone* which was a massive lump of gritstone set up about waist height. The crushed rock and were was taken to the washers.

In the seventeenth and eighteenth centuries washing was done almost entirely by the women. They worked in small groups employed by a master washer who made a contract with the miners or the owner and paid the washers by piece rate. The washers stood at a tub or dolly (hence the domestic dolly-tub) full of water. They held a round sieve by two handles and a girl or boy *server* lifted a shovelful of bouse into the sieve. This was then jerked up and down in the water in such a skilled way that ore sank to the bottom of the bouse on the sieve and the finer ore went through the sieve into the tub. Stone and waste was scraped off the top of the sieve leaving small lumps of ore and mixed ore and rock in the bottom layers. The manipulation of the sieve was extremely hard work leaning over the tub from which water splashed and it kept the women's clothes saturated to the waist. Some companies provided their washers with heavy flannel petticoats but whether or not with their greater weight they were any comfort only a washer could say. The washing was done at the shaft head, on the high and wild moors and fells, fully exposed to wind and weather, and a crippling rheumatism could be the only end of such exposure. In 1720 women washers on one Yorkshire mine, typical of most, were paid 3d or 4d a day. On that mine miners were then getting 8d to 14d a day.

Washing was largely mechanised in the early nineteenth century and became a man's job. On a mine group in 1683 there were 20 miners mostly working in pairs but there was one partnership listed as "Stoney and ptns", probably of four men or three men and a boy. Among them they produced 3056 horse loads of cleaned ore (the horse load was 2 cwts) in six months. Ten carriers were employed to carry this ore to the smelt mill. The carriage of ore was done by a pack-horse along tracks which can still be found. It provided what was probably the healthiest job on the mines. Ore was stacked at the mill and at some smelt mills women were employed to barrow it in as required and also to barrow in peat or other fuel. A common form used in the lists is that a woman and her daughter were employed to work together, and this persisted until far into the nineteenth century.

Until well into the eighteenth century, and in many mills right to the end of mining, the ore was smelted in the ore hearth. This was a furnace very like a large blacksmith's hearth, though with a shallow trough bottom. Ore and fuel were piled on the hearth and a high temperature got by means of water-wheel driven bellows. During a full run or shift, *stint* or *core*, ore and fuel were added at the smelter's discretion and at an early stage a partly fused mass of ore, slag and cinder was formed which the smelter moved about in the fire according to the temperature which was required at different parts of the process. This was done with a heavy poker which if too long would have been too heavy to manipulate. So the smelter had to work near the fire, using the poker in exhausting heat at the front with a cold draught on his back. At some stages red hot masses of partly smelted ore were raked out onto the "workstone", a narrow shelf on the front of the hearth, and worked up there before being placed back into a special place in the fire.

As lead was released from the ore it ran out of the hearth into a large pot placed to received it, and then while still liquid was lifted out with an iron ladle to be poured into moulds in which it cooled to form *pieces*. These were approximately one hundred weight so that two would form a normal load for a pack-horse. The large pig of about 10cwt was not cast until carts became the common means of transport about the end of the eighteenth century. Every part of the work at the hearth was exceedingly heavy and was done close up to a fierce, open fire and a mass of molten metal. Fumes were given off by the molten lead and, although these in theory were carried off by a canopy and flue, many hung about and lead poisoning was a serious risk which the smelter had to face.

The reverberatory furnace introduced by the London (Quaker) Lead Company in the eighteenth century was a closed furnace, very much larger, heated by a separate fireplace. Ore was fed onto the bed of the furnace from a hopper in the top and manipulation of the ore was done with pokers, through small doors in the sides. The furnace had a high chimney at the end opposite to the fire which caused the draught and drew away all the fumes. The glare of the furnace was much less than that from the ore hearth, but tools were generally heavier and larger and the quantities of metal produced were much larger. On the whole the conditions in the larger reverberatory smelting mills were better than with the ore hearths, but work was still very heavy and the smelter had the violent contrast between this hot and confined working conditions and his long walk home through all kinds of weather.

Conditions of work were inseparably connected with earnings, living conditions and recreation. It was the outstanding character of lead mining that the productivity of a vein was subject to violent and completely unpredictable fluctuation. A vein might in one part carry a rib of ore that would give a rich return for working but equally it might change to a portion with little or no ore in it, in which there was no return at all. These frequent variations were the only constant and predictable feature of a vein. There was a constant urge to search for new veins, to try one's luck in a new trial and to change one's *bargain* or working place. The richest vein might in a yard change to barren spar, and of course the opposite might also happen and sudden rich ore be found. It was this gamble that a rich place might lie only a few yards ahead that tempted the miner to keep on however poor his place might be showing. Wages were based upon a payment according to the amount of ore raised and could involve periods of absolute poverty, only survived on loans or *advances* made against the possibility of a good *strike*. A life of uncertainty with frequent and recurrent periods of debt and near starvation was all too common among a large proportion of the miners.

A more secure job, though with wages not much more than subsistence, was that of men on *dead* work. That is driving levels, cross cuts or adits through rock and not along a vein, where no ore was encountered unless a hitherto unknown vein was found. Payment for dead work was usually made per fathom cut, with adjustments for the hardness of the rock, or a particular length might be let to a partnership or contractor. The extreme cases of course were the long adits which were driven towards the end of the eighteenth century and in the nineteenth. Some of these long adits, only possible to a big company with plenty of resources were a few miles in length, two or three miles being common, and some being four or even five miles. Some took as long as thirty years to complete and an experienced driver could spend a good part of his working life on one or perhaps two adits, with a fairly steady sure wage.

Other men with wage rate pay were the level archers and timber men who supported the main levels or *waygates* of the mine with masonry arches or timber framing. There was always some variation even in the more regulated wages as the custom of monthly or three monthly bargaining allowed some adjustment of rates to the notoriously variable price of lead on the markets. It is a fairly true generalisation to say that the people who made money out of lead mining were the merchants and the larger owner-operating companies who had their royalties and dividends whenever the mine was in good ore. The great houses of the Devonshires and the Beaumonts, the London and country houses of Bathurst, Denys and other mine-owning families are in violent contrast with the poverty-stricken hovels of their miners on the coalfields and in the lead dales.

One result of this arduous life of the miner was that such recreation as he could get was taken vigorously whether in the form of sport, in the brass band, or in work for his chapel. Shortage of food drove many to be skilled and persistent poachers to the benefit both of their family's diet and their health, and there are few but the land-owning class who would attach any blame to this activity. Hunting, represented by hound trailing, a course being set by trailing an aniseed-soaked rag across the country, was a popular sport for which the miners from time to time took a day off work. A whole mine would turn out for such an event. Tan Hill was the chosen place for Swaledale miners to witness and perhaps take part in prize fights, boxing and wrestling matches, and some famous bouts were promoted there in the eighteenth century.

On quieter occasions holidays were marked by dancing, both mixed country style and clog dancing among the men. The occasion of the annual fairs, particularly the Batholomew (Bartle) Fair at Reeth, drew all the dale together for a day of jollity, meeting old friends, buying new (often second-hand) clothes as far as one could, seeing fairings, dancing and often a good deal of drinking towards night. All these recreations however were only occasional gleams in a hard and dreary life and they serve mainly to show up the indomitable spirit of the miners and their wives, which could survive poverty, uncertainty and danger with only these rare times of jollity.

(Yorkshire Annual 1973)

SPIRIT
OF THE DALES

Curlews, Ingleborough

Godfrey Wilson

SPIRIT OF THE DALES

The long story of man's life in the Dales has revealed the steady evolution of a community with some features in the character of its people and in their dialect, that mark them as worthy of a distinctive and descriptive name. To call a man a Dalesman (remembering that the title is bi-sexual and includes Daleswoman) implies not only his origin, upbringing and immediate environment within the Pennine dales, but imputes to him some recognisable habits of life and thought. The Pennines are a large area and it is possible to distinguish the people of the Yorkshire Dales from those of Durham or Derbyshire by some traits in their character and in their folk speech and folk lore, as well as in their geographical location and their history. Without pursuing these distinctions we may ask what are the particular qualities that go to make up the Yorkshire Dalesman.

The dialect that he speaks is properly a matter for the etymologist and the grammarian; suffice it to say that the Norse invaders who left us a rich vocabulary were far more numerous in the mid-Pennine Dales than they were either to north or south, and their enrichment of the local speech is strongly evident in both dialect and place-names. The rough topography, the hard climate and the virtual isolation from the outside world through many centuries are shared by all the dales and have contributed to the breeding of a basic Pennine character; but the thin and scttered nature of much of the population that lies between the two great cross routes of the Aire Gap and Stainmore, the likelihood of being quite cut off in winter storms and floods, the prevalence of high ground and the general difficulty of communication between one dale and the next, have bred a people among whom an almost aggressive self-sufficiency and independence are expected and valued qualities.

A person lacking these qualities is said to he "slack set up", "slammoky" or would by my grandmother have been described as "summat an nowt, wants a nurse, shoo does". There is a score of other terms for such persons. This self-reliance does nothing to reduce the instant and unstinted help given quietly, efficiently and without fuss in any emergency as soon as it is known. Dalesfolk are afraid of fuss and distrust it. They are slow-spoken, given to hiding their emotions and always wedded to understatement. A man in robust health would be most likely to say he "wor noan so bad" and that might also be his verdict on his wife's special effort in cookery, he feeling that he had given high praise. "I'm nobbut middling" or "I'm raither poorly" could be the reply of a person very ill or not far from death. One might hope to detect no more than a proper avoidance of over-praise when, after critical and weighty consideration, it is said of a piece of work that "it mud (might) a been warr (worse)"; and an emotional parting is sometimes avoided with "Nah, tak care o' thysen, owd lad". This use of "owd lad" or "lad" is properly a mark of affection widely and sincerely bestowed between friends, and has little reference to age. It would not be used to describe a person but only in address to one.

The Dalesman has a deep and often partly concealed sense of humour, frequently with a grim turn or touched with something of the macabre. His quick wit in repartee has the same flavour. All this is a reflection of the age-old struggle against a tough environment in which living means constant effort. He is a hard bargainer and is careful, even "near", in money matters, but again this is a product of making a living that is possible only by hard work and constant watchfulness amid conditions that often appear adverse. The true Dalesman has integrity and, like Wycliffe, holds his "unswerving convictions", often mistakenly described as obstinacy by those who know him least well. Withal, he has generosity and a great impulse to hospitality. These qualities are blended with an intense local pride and love and loyalty to his dale, never flaunted but always there, a part of his nature.

In recent decades this distinctive character has been challenged, for it is being subjected to considerable pressure by the impact of a different culture. It is a multi-headed attack. The popularity of the motor car has brought thousands of townspeople into the Dales, visitors, mostly for a few hours only, attracted by the scenery so well advertised by the travel agents. Quiet villages win admiration and by their admirers are made unquiet. Car drivers enjoy exploring narrow by-roads and soon create the conditions that call for their widening. There is also increasing demand for weekend and holiday cottages, and now in summer whenever the weather is good there is an invasion vastly greater than any previously experienced in the history of the Dales. Like their predecessors, these invaders bring with them an alien culture – this time an urban one; and this the media supplement with their popularisation of habits and tastes imported from the wider world. How are the Dales and their communities reacting to this last invasion? How can they still preserve the things that have attracted the invaders – unspoiled natural scenery, undisturbed villages and a highly individual way of life created by many centuries of slow evolution?

Dalesfolk live in the valleys but look to the hills – the hills that are always there, symbols of stability and permanence, not changing noticeably within a long human life. On the hills, quiet and healing solitude can be found after the exertion of the climb. Among those of the Dales population who will accept and serve the expanding demands of the invaders, there is a growing nucleus of those who will fight to preserve the qualities of their rural way of life that have matured through many centuries, are rooted in the Dales environment, and strongly ingrained in the people through many generations.

The physical Dales may be scarred by quarries and blanketed in parts by monotonous plantations of conifers, made noisy by busy roads and crowded car parks, but they are large enough to bear these scars even as they regret them. Some of the Dalesfolk both old and young will still look to and go to the hills. They will seek rest and quiet contemplation, as they absorb the broad spread of the country they love. They will gather peace and refreshment of body, mind and spirit. This section of the "native" Dalesfolk will meet all the challenges and changes that are bound to come, and there is increasing evidence that their love of the Dales is as great as that which Dalesmen have held in the past. They will, like their forebears, hesitate to speak of and define the Spirit of the Dales, but they will live in it and it will be preserved to serve and inspire future generations, as it has been the inspiring force in the past. May it be so.

(from *Open Fell Hidden Dale* – photographs by John & Eliza Forder;
Frank Peters Publishing Ltd, 1985)

INDEX

Accrington 37, 40
Addingham 19, 50, 81, 83, 131
Aire, river 89
Airedale 20, 23
Airton 53
Aldborough 131
Alston 133
Appersett 37
Appleby-in-Westmorland 120–1
Appletreewick 52, 81, 84, 117, 133, 137–8
Arkengarthdale 19, 34, 39, 40, 132
Arncliffe 83, 96
Askrigg 50, 62, 89, 98, 121

Bain, river 37
Bainbridge 19, 37–8, 39, 40, 117, 121
Barden 34, 37, 38, 40, 50, 91, 92, 117–22, 127
Barnsley 68
Beverley 112
Bierley 136
Bingley 72, 99, 114
Bishopdale 40, 133
Blackstone Edge 19, 62
Blubberhouses 19, 83
Bolling Hall, Bradford 104
Bolton Abbey 50, 63
Bolton by Bowland 107
Bolton Priory 19, 20, 38, 52, 66, 76, 79, 89, 90, 92, 108, 117, 118, 120, 127, 138
Boroughbridge 135
Bowes 19
Bowland, forest of 20, 34, 37, 40, 132, 133
Bradford 69, 79, 83
Bramham 88
Bridlington 53
Brimham 52
Brough, Cumbria 50, 121
Brough, Humberside 135
Brougham Castle 121
Broughton 101
Buckden 37, 117, 121, 141
Burley 83
Burnley 82
Burnsall 90, 114, 115, 116
Burtersett 37, 108
Burton Agnes 53

Calder Valley 81, 84
Cam Fell 19
Carperby 62, 98
Castle Bolton 88–9
Castley 77
Catterick 66, 88, 92
Colne Valley 81
Coniston Cold 81, 83
Conistone 90
Cononley 83, 141
Countersett 108
Coverdale 62, 98
Clapham 20, 91
Cracoe 53
Craven, district 19, 20, 21, 22, 26, 69, 81, 83, 99, 103, 117, 132
Cross Hills 83

Dacre 38–9, 83, 134
Darley 83
Dent 22, 72, 116
Dentdale 23, 62, 72
Dodworth 68
Doncaster 126
Draughton 50, 81
Drebley 117, 118, 119, 120
Durham 91

Earby 83
Easby 78
Eastby 83
Elslack 91, 106
Embsay 76, 79, 83

Farnhill 69, 104
Fewston 140
Flasby 81, 126
Fountains Abbey 19, 20, 32, 33, 38, 52, 66, 76–7, 81, 113
Fraisthorpe 53

Gargrave 20, 21, 81, 82, 90, 113, 114
Garsdale 72
Giggleswick 22, 73, 101, 114–5, 116
Gisburn 52, 117

Glusburn   99
Grassington   20, 21–2, 30, 32, 33, 72,
    80, 101, 111, 124, 133, 135–6, 137,
    138–9, 140–1, 143
Greenhow   22, 63, 131, 135, 136, 141,
    143

Halifax   21, 40, 81, 104, 120
Hallamshire   36
Halton Gill   22
Hanlith   81, 126
Hampsthwaite   83, 131
Hardraw   62
Hartwith   83
Hawes   23, 62, 98
Healaugh   146
Hebden   53–4, 67, 81, 126, 135, 141,
    142–3
Helwith Bridge   20, 59–60, 91, 103
Holme on Spalding   136
Horton in Ribblesdale   22, 23, 59, 103
Hubberholme   91
Huddersfield   136
Hull   23
Humber, river   134, 135

Ilkley   52, 73, 114, 115
Ingleton   20, 23, 90
Ivelet   22

Jervaulx Abbey   38

Keighley   69, 81
Keld   62, 98
Kendal   21
Keswick   140
Kettlewell   35, 83, 133, 141
Kildwick   22, 69, 79, 83, 89, 101
Kilnsey   19, 20, 22, 66, 81, 121, 141
Kirkby Lonsdale   89
Kirkby Malham   53, 81, 83, 101, 107,
    114, 115
Kirkby Malzeard   21
Kirkstall   32, 88, 140
Knaresborough   20, 34, 38, 39, 40, 83,
    117

Lancaster   20, 91
Langcliffe   83, 84
Langstrothdale   34, 35, 37, 40, 98, 117
Leathley   76
Leeds   21, 69, 79, 81, 83
Leeds and Liverpool Canal   21, 69, 82
Linton   80, 81, 83, 90, 92, 114, 126,
    128, 140
Litton   52, 77, 101, 117

Littondale   19
Liverpool   80
Long Preston   50, 114
Low Moor   136
Low Row   98
Lune, river   40

Malham   19, 20, 22, 23, 52, 57, 66, 69,
    97, 121, 141
Mallerstang   98, 121
Manchester   21
Marrick   135
Marske   89
Masham   40
Middleham   22
Muker   62

Newcastle-upon-Tyne   91
Newsham   81
Nidderdale   38–9, 40, 52, 57, 83
Norton Conyers   124, 125
Norton Tower   117, 124–8

Old Gang Mine, Swaledale   52, 145–6
Otley   114, 115–6
Ouse, river   20
Oxton   52

Pateley Bridge   20, 83, 135
Paythorne   42
Pendragon Castle   121
Pendle, forest of   34, 37, 40
Penistone   108
Penyghent   22
Pickering   66
Pontefract   126
Pudsey   104

Quernmore   58

Rathmell   101
Reeth   40, 150
Ribble, river   20, 22
Ribblehead   22, 23
Ribblesdale   20, 52, 57, 59, 97
Richmond   37, 38, 40, 63, 77–8, 91,
    114
Richmondshire   36
Riddlesden Hall   108
Rigton   38, 76
Rimington   52, 132–3
Ripley   131, 135
Ripon   112
Rossendale, forest of   37, 40
Rylstone   124, 125, 126, 127

Salterforth   23
Sawley, North Yorkshire   77
Sawley Abbey   19, 20, 52, 77, 89
Sedbergh   114, 116
Settle   19, 20, 21, 23, 69, 73, 83, 121
Sheffield   69, 108, 110, 140
Shipley   69, 99
Silsden   76, 90
Skipton   21, 35, 50, 81, 82, 83, 114,
    117, 120, 121, 124, 125
Slaidburn   37, 114, 116
Spofforth   103
Stainforth   20, 22, 52, 101
Stainmore   40
Stapleton   88
Starbotton   62, 121, 141
Steeton   81
Stockton   133
Storith   79
Stump Cross   22
Swale, river   22, 88, 135
Swaledale   40, 52, 62, 131, 132, 133,
    135, 136, 145–7

Tan Hill   149
Tees, river   135
Thorn   42
Thornborough   42
Thorner   42
Thorngumbald   42
Thornhill   42
Thornholme   42
Thornthwaite   42

Thornton   42, 90
Thornton-in-Craven   42
Thornton in Lonsdale   42
Thornton-le-Beans   42
Thornton-le-Clay   42
Thornton-le-Street   42
Threshfield   47, 50, 80, 81, 93, 114,
    115, 124, 126, 128
Tong   102
Trawden, forest of   36, 37, 39, 40

Victoria Cave, Settle   57

Wakefield   21, 79, 81
Washburn, river   23, 50, 83
Watendlath   20
Wensleydale   23, 26, 37–8, 40, 57, 61,
    62, 72, 91, 96, 98, 104, 117, 121, 133
West End   50, 83
Wharfe   20
Wharfe, river   75, 90
Wharfedale   19, 30, 38, 46, 50, 57, 61,
    63, 66, 72, 96, 98, 143
Whernside   58
Whitewell   37
Wigglesworth   108

Yarm   21, 135
Yockenthwaite   22
York   20, 21, 23, 53, 66, 67, 77, 87–8,
    112, 133